# ON THE 4:33

A One-Year Journey of A Life in Transition

By
Salvatore Petrosino

---

**"On the 4:33"** is a reference to when I would text my wife, Carol, every day after work to let her know I was on the 4:33 pm train out of Penn Station heading to our new home in Manalapan, New Jersey. I would ask how her day was going and what we were doing for dinner. Were we going out or was she cooking? I would try to communicate this before the train left the station and entered the tunnel where phone service would be cut off until we reemerged from the bowels of the underground and were back outside heading toward my destination, the Matawan-Aberdeen train station. During the hour and ten minutes on the train, I would use this time to read, review student scripts, or simply, rest. Once arriving at the station, I would get in my car and drive another fifteen minutes before finally arriving home. The new house has a circular driveway and after moving from Brooklyn where it would take me a half-hour to find a parking place, I appreciate simply getting out of the car and heading inside.

That journey home is a good metaphor for where I am now. On September 5th, 2019, Carol, my wife of nearly thirty-eight years, had a sudden heart attack, went into a coma, and never woke up. Since then, I find myself still in a tunnel, only this time I am on an unknown journey heading toward a destination that has yet to be revealed.

I have decided to write a journal to explore more deeply the many emotions and challenges I am experiencing and try to get a better understanding of my place in front of them. I don't want to go through this terrible time in a pedestrian way, I want to at *least*, try to understand the *why* and *what* I am experiencing in this new and unexpected reality.

I don't know where I'm headed as I begin this new journey. Perhaps writing this journal is simply part of a bigger journey I am meant to be on, a necessary step toward better understanding myself and learning the lessons I need to learn to find the path I am meant to be on.

As someone who has written a few scripts and taught young filmmakers to come from a truthful place and share their voice, I intend to heed that advice and share my own experiences, challenges, discoveries, and the lessons I learn along the way to wherever I'm headed. Thus, I begin this journal.

# The Prelude:
# End of Summer 2019

In the waning days of August, Carol had been complaining more than in the past about the severity of her panic attacks. They seemed to be getting worse. For years, she battled anxiety and fought through these attacks, which ranged from passing to severe. Eight years ago, the day after we celebrated my fifty-fifth birthday, Carol woke me in the middle of the night and told me she was having difficulty breathing. I called an ambulance and when we arrived at Methodist Hospital, she collapsed. The next image I saw was a team of doctors suddenly working frantically on her, placing a tube down her throat and rushing her out of the emergency room. I remember not fully comprehending what was going on, feeling that what was happening was surreal. What wasn't surreal was realizing at that moment, she might die. I remember asking myself, "How did this happen? It was 3:00 a.m. Should I call my daughter and son or wait?" Fortunately, Carol recovered. She was diagnosed with pneumonia and after a short stay at the hospital; she was back home, shaken by the experience but alive.

Perhaps this is a good time to give you a perspective on who Carol was, and how she is remembered by those who were lucky enough to know her and have her in their lives. She was a devoted wife, an amazing mother and friend, and what you call *"a tough cookie."* However, she always maintained her class, which was one of the first things that attracted me to her. No matter what she wore, it would always look good on her five foot -seven frame. She had short, thick shoulder length black hair, and the hands and feet of a model.

Carol had a tough childhood. She experienced significant trauma and loss as she grew up, which was the root cause of the anxiety she later developed. When she was nine, her four-year old sister, Marietta developed scarlet fever. Tragically, she was given medication she was allergic to without being properly tested, and it caused her to have a seizure. Without oxygen to her brain for an extended period of time, Marietta suffered damage to eighty-five percent of her brain and was bed-ridden for the rest of her twenty-eight years on this planet. The family sued the hospital but, as Carol explained, the doctors covered for each other. Then, when Carol was sixteen, her father passed after a short battle with cancer. Before she was twenty-eight, she also lost her mother, who passed from a heart attack.

On top of grieving her mother, Carol also took on the responsibility of caring for her sister- feeding and dressing her and attending to all her needs, which were significant. Some people suggested placing Marietta in a home, but Carol wouldn't hear of it. She devoted her time and sacrificed a good part of her late twenties and early thirties taking care of her sister.

I first met Carol in 1976 at a neighbor's Communion party for their daughter. I remember not wanting to go, but my parents thought it would be disrespectful if I didn't at least stop by. I remember seeing Carol for the first time. She was wearing a brown dress and looked great. I stayed for the entire party. Carol was the type of traditional woman who you knew if you started getting serious with, you would eventually marry. In 1981, after dating for nearly five years, we were married. There were those who questioned why I would place myself in such a challenging situation where

4

I would also take on the responsibility of caring for her sister. My answer was always, "I love Marietta," and being with a woman with that capacity to love, made me love Carol even more.

Two weeks before her heart attack, when she started getting panic attacks again, I remember one particular moment after she walked up the stairs. She was feeling short-winded and asked me if I thought it was pneumonia again. I told her most likely not, but to be sure schedule an appointment with the doctor. She adamantly refused. In fact, we argued about it.

How often have we heard stories where if only the person would have listened and gone to the doctor they would still be here? This moment easily lends itself to reflection and frustration. Why didn't she listen? I ask myself, "Why didn't I just pick her up over my shoulder and take her to the doctor? " How many times did I, my daughter, Danielle, and son, Chris, ask her, plead with her to go to a doctor? We all have free will and make choices that are not always correct. You simply cannot look back with regret. It serves no one. Regret is destructive, will pummel you and prevent you from ever moving forward.

A week later, on August 20, Carol called me at the office to tell me she'd just had her worst panic attack ever. It would be revealed later that this was not a panic attack, but a minor heart attack.

## Labor Day Weekend

Little did we know this would be the last holiday we would all share together as a family. As always, everyone came to our home. Traditionally, Carol and I would go shopping days before and buy enough food to last a month. We would always go back and forth as to how much to buy. Our new home in Jersey has a beautiful backyard and pool, a perfect setting for an end-of-summer celebration. Plus both Chris and Danielle live less than fifteen minutes away.

5

I still see the images of smiling faces of family and friends sharing that day, as if I'm watching an old super-8 movie. When I reflect on that day, oddly enough the one thing I remember most is the group picture. There we are, some twenty of us setting up for a traditional family group picture and once again, Carol and I are standing in the background. Seems every group picture we have taken, no matter where we are, Carol and I are in the background. I remember saying just before the picture was taken, that I wanted us to move to the front of the group. Too late, the picture taken, the moment passed. I wish we had moved to the front because you can barely see us, especially Carol, in the picture.

I would see that picture posted on Instagram and Facebook the next day from several friends who were at the house, smiling faces, enjoying life, enjoying each other but it will be that group picture I remember most. I think this is a good representation of our life as a couple: family and friends celebrating together for a wonderful life moment at our home with us in the background. It's a symbolic memory to serve as our last picture together.

## September 4: The Day Before The Heart Attack

What I remember about our last day together are visual snippets. Danielle is at the house coming by after work to pick up my grandson Aiden, who just turned four, and my two–year-old granddaughter, Aubrey Lynn. Carol would babysit Aiden and Aubrey four days a week and Danielle would sometimes stay for dinner, which always made us happy. When I arrive at the house, dinner is already on the table. Carol had a great way of timing our dinner so it would be done as I arrived home. I never could have imagined this would be our last meal together.

After dinner, Danielle and the kids leave, and Carol tells me we need to go shopping to pickup salmon because Danielle and the kids are eating over again tomorrow. We head out to Wegmans, a popular food chain in

New Jersey but not popular with Carol, who thought they were pricey and didn't have the name brands she preferred. We used to go back and forth about shopping there, as I liked the diversity of food products and the large layout. As we drive to the store, she teases me and says, "We're going to your favorite store." The only reason we are going this time is because Carol does like their fish. I pick out four beautiful pieces of salmon. This is a moment I would never have recalled if it hadn't turned out to be the last time we ever went shopping together.

As we head home, Carol asks if I wouldn't mind stopping at Rita's for some Italian ice and ice cream. Although I'm tired, I say, "Sure," because I know Carol needs to get out of the house after being home all day. I give her the ice she wants and go back for mine. I turn around and look at her. I can still see Carol sitting on the passenger's side eating her ice. Another simple, non-descript moment that has become so prominent in my mind and now in my heart. How I wish I could go back to that moment and change *everything*.

## September 5

I remember the morning of September 5 so clearly, so visually. The alarm goes off and as I gradually wake up, Carol sits up from her side of the bed, with her back to me and says her foot is hurting again. A few months back, her foot was so badly sprained she could barely walk on it. She pauses, frustrated, and tells me, "*Just when I'm starting to feel good, now my foot hurts!*" I reassure her that it's something we can take care of and I tell her to make an appointment to visit the Emergency Care doctor who helped her last time or make an appointment to see the podiatrist.

That was to be our last conversation in person. When I think about this, it's so appropriate in a way. I always understood Carol had a challenging childhood and her history programmed her to expect the worse. We had spoken about this often during our life together. She was accustomed to tragedy and, as a defense mechanism, was always preparing for the worst-case scenario. It limited her in that she never truly allowed herself to exhale for a long period of time without feeling vulnerable or expecting something bad was just around the corner.

Carol and I had many joyous times in our lives, and I would always be happy whenever I saw her happy at these moments, relaxed, smiling, and embracing the beauty of life. In reflection, throughout our marriage, I tried to help Carol feel peaceful and not grow anxious or worried about things. Her being peaceful and happy was a goal I tried hard to help her achieve. During these times, she would often say, "I wish I could have your sense of peace," and I would always respond, "You can." I don't remember much after that brief morning conversation, only that she was upset and frustrated.

My next memory of that morning, after telling Carol to make an appointment to see the doctor is being on the New Jersey train heading to New York Penn Station. I am sitting with my friend Nick, who I met when I first started taking the NJ train from the Matawan-Aberdeen train station. I always try to get the corner seats that face each other so we can speak more directly. As I am talking with Nick, my cellphone rings. It's Carol. She never calls me when I'm heading to work so my first instinct is that she is anxious about her foot. She tells me she made a doctor's appointment at Urgent Care for her foot for 4:30 p.m., after she is finished babysitting. I tell her I will leave work early to take her.

Twenty minutes later, Carol calls again. This time she sounds anxious and says she called Danielle and my daughter–in–law Melissa, and told them she couldn't baby-sit. For Carol to do this, I know she is truly not feeling well. I ask her what's wrong and she tells me she is feeling very anxious and wishes I were with her. Thinking she is having another panic attack, my natural reaction is to do what I have done so many times before, try to calm her down. She tells me she will call me back.

What I don't know at this time is Carol is having heart-attack symptoms. The conversation with Carol on the train, telling me she wishes I was with her, stings deeply now and I play that moment often. How could I have known she was heading for a heart attack? If I was with her, I could have helped in some way, calmed her down, let the paramedics in, taken her to the hospital. Maybe those few extra minutes would have saved her. Did I ask her if she wanted me to come home? I honestly don't remember. Do I not remember because it hurts too much? I am at peace with at least one thing: I never for a moment thought Carol was in a critical life-threatening situation.

## The Call

I'm in my office and at 10:54, I receive a call from Carol. She tells me something is terribly wrong. I can tell from the tension in her voice she is in crisis. My initial reflex is to once again try to calm her down but my instincts tell me this is more than just a panic attack and she is in real distress. I tell her to call an ambulance and that I'm on my way home. She says she is going to call which tells me this is serious. She tells me, " *I think this is it. Goodbye, Sal.*" The words hit me like an overhand punch. Time abruptly stops, my brain is stunned, and every part of my body goes numb, life never to be the same. I ask her why she is saying that and once again tell her to call an ambulance, but she is already in the process of hanging up. I can only imagine the anxiety and fear she was feeling at that moment.

Never did I think those words would be the last Carol would ever speak to me. Did she know she was having a heart attack? Did she truly believe she was going to die? It pains me to know she was alone and afraid and I wasn't there to hold her, help her, save her.

9

I would find out later that Carol had also called Danielle that morning, who also thought she was having another panic attack and tried calming her down. Carol then called her closest friend Linda, at 11:13 a.m. She told Linda she missed Carroll Street, the street where she lived her entire life, and wished her mother were here. Her last words to Linda were that she loved her and had to go.

## The Train Ride Back Home

I race out of the office and head to Penn Station on 31st Street and 7th Avenue. It normally takes me eighteen to twenty-minutes to walk from my office on 23rd and 3rd to the station. I check my NJ Transit app. There is an 11:20 a.m. train. I have just enough time to race and catch that train but it's going to be tight.

I'm outside and start walking at a fast pace. Taking a cab in the city at this time is ludicrous and I would never catch the train. After making this walk back and forth from the office for over a year, I'm in shape and my wind is good. However, my legs unexpectedly begin to feel like cement halfway to the station. I assume it's stress and keep moving.

I call Melissa, who lives in Matawan, about a fifteen-minute drive to the house. I am happy to get her on the first ring and she is already in the car, out shopping with my grandson Anthony. I tell her Carol called me and is in distress and that an ambulance is on its way. I ask her if she can go to the house and let me know what's going on. She tells me she is on her way.

I am now a block away from Penn Station and see the time on the Madison Square Garden clock. 11:18 a.m. I have three minutes to get inside Penn Station and find the track the train is leaving from. The trains always wait an extra minute before departing. Luckily, it's track 2, right where I enter. I race down the stairs and get on the train with about a minute to spare. I can feel my breathing is strained. I don't know if this is because

I was walking fast or stress. I attribute it to both. The doors close and the train departs. When a train leaves Penn Station, it spends the first seven minutes or so in a tunnel and communication is just about impossible. I convince myself this short time will allow me to catch my breath before I call Melissa.

The train leaves the station, and we are literally *crawling*! This feels like one of those nightmares where you want to get to a certain place but you can only move in slow motion. It is at this moment that I start getting a bad feeling about how this is going and thinking "*This is already written in destiny's script.*"

The train continues puttering along. I figure at this pace, it will take me an hour and twenty minutes to arrive at the Matawan-Aberdeen station, which should be around 12:40 p.m. Normally, an express train takes a little over an hour. We are finally out of the tunnel. I wait five more minutes and call Melissa. By this time, she should just about be at the house. She picks up and tells me in a nervous voice that she is on Westbrook Way and can see a number of ambulances at the house. My immediate thought is, "*OK Carol listened to me and called an ambulance.*" But my next thought is, "*Why are there a number of ambulances?* She tells me she will call me back.

The train is incredibly slow and almost feels like it is stopping. I feel myself growing more and more anxious. I can walk faster and get to the house. I remember thinking "*Isn't it outrageous that in all the times I have traveled on this line, today, at the most critical moment, the train is going the slowest it has ever gone?*" I start to think again, "*This is a bad omen.*"

I remember when my brother, Frank, was killed in a motorcycle accident while I was driving home from the dentist and, for some reason, I took a different path. If I had traveled the route I always took, I would have driven right past the accident scene. I question why I am thinking of that moment with my brother at this time? I don't like where this is heading. Less than two minutes later, I receive a phone call from Linda. When Carol had called her earlier that morning and told her something was seriously wrong, Linda and her husband, Kenny, drove to the house to check on her. Linda tells me she and Kenny are at the house. I ask her how Carol is doing. I visualize the doctors' giving her oxygen and perhaps a sedative to calm her down. Linda says the words that will echo with me for as long as I live, *"They're having a hard time resuscitating her."* The words penetrate like a sudden stab of a bayonet in my stomach. There is no warning for this, no preparation or protection. The body and mind instinctively react to the shock and you have no choice but to become its victim.

I don't remember if I pause or respond quickly but the first word that comes out my mouth expresses my sheer disbelief. *"What?"* I can't comprehend how we went from a moment when Carol's foot hurt to a life -and-death moment. As human beings, I don't think we're made to absorb this type of shock. How can you go from one reality to another...in an *instant*? The answer is you can't.

Combat soldiers, who see horrific acts not meant for humans to see, are forever scarred emotionally and psychologically. What I don't know at the time, alone on a slow-moving train, is in that horrible moment, life as I know it has ended. My reality altered forever. So many thoughts race through my head on that train ride as I try to fathom the magnitude of what was just conveyed to me.

I wait for Linda to respond, and she does. *"They're trying to resuscitate her but she's not coming to, they won't allow us in the house."* I don't remember much after that with the possible exception of me thinking, *"Are you fucking kidding?"* She tells me she will call me back.

I sit on the train and actually feel my blood rushing to my head and my heart palpitating. I am numb. I try to comprehend what Linda said. My eyes begin to tear and the woman sitting two seats from me gives me a quick glance and turns her eyes away. This is a nightmare I am living, alone on a slow-moving train trying to get to my wife who is fighting for her life.

How in God's name did this happen out of nowhere, so quickly? My mind races in a slow-motion reality.

I don't remember much about the rest of the train ride with the exception of Kenny calling me about twenty minutes later to tell me the paramedics were taking Carol to Robert Woods Johnson Hospital in New Brunswick and that they would meet me there. A rush of questions and thoughts races through my head. I think about what this might mean. I try *not* to think what this might mean. Do my kids know yet? Should I call them? Of course I should call them, a stupid thought. I Google the hospital name and put it in my Waze app so I can place it in my car's navigation system and immediately head to the hospital as soon as I get off the train.

*FINALLY*, the train stops at Matawan-Aberdeen. I race to my car, put the address in the navigation, and I'm on my way. It's been about forty minutes since I last spoke with Linda. I call her and she tells me they are waiting in the emergency room. What am I going to find when I get to the hospital? Will Carol be OK? Will I be able to see her? Talk with her? Will she be alert? Can she talk?

When I reflect on that train ride from hell, I believe it is the first time in my life where I felt challenged in every way a human being can be tested. So many thoughts and questions raced through my mind during the one- and- a- half hours. Is this a pre-written script? Pre-destined? Is there anything I could have done to change it?

I enter the hospital's emergency room and see Linda, Kenny, Melissa and my grandson Anthony in a small waiting room. I gather a quick read and they all look concerned but not overly somber. I get a piece of the story from each of them. Carol's heart stopped twice when the paramedics were at the house. Once they got her heart beating the second time, they took her to the hospital. I try to stay with the positive that they got her heart going. I wonder how long it was in between her heart stopping and restarting?

How much time had passed without oxygen going to her brain? That will be the key.

There is another woman in the room who cautiously walks over to me and in a low, reserved voice (or is it solemn?) and tells me she is a minister and asks if I want to talk, pray, or have her give last rites. Last rites? What? What does she know that we don't? Is this woman *always* here, or is she here specifically because of Carol's condition and knows something we don't? Linda hears the woman's questions and we look at each other trying to mask our worst fears. I tell the woman, not at this moment.

Linda tells me she called Danielle who had been driving from work to pick up Aiden from school and was heading home to relieve her mother-in-law who was watching Aubrey. My son, Chris, walks in and I can tell he wasn't told Carol's heart stopped twice. He asks me how's she's doing and each of us in the room give him an update.

A young emergency room doctor walks in and asks for Carol's husband. I approach him and introduce myself. I try to get a read on his expression. I focus on every word, every syllable, to get some clarity but it's all going by too fast. I gather my thoughts, and try to continue reading him while he is speaking. As he continues giving us information about what happened, and where her current state is, my instincts are once again telling me this is not good, not going in the direction I was praying for on the train.

He confirms Carol had a heart attack at the house and her heart stopped twice. The paramedics got her heart going but he says her heart stopped again in the ambulance but they were able to re-start it again. This would later be disputed by the hospital. Why it wasn't clear if she had another heart attack in the ambulance is to say the least, perplexing. If she did have a third heart attack, what role did it play? He also tells me that in the process of trying to revive her, the paramedics cracked two of Carol's ribs.

The doctor tells me they placed Carol in a thermo-blanket that reduces a person's body temperature to just above freezing in order to slow down brain damage. The words "brain damage" stop everything. Brain damage!? I don't believe a person can fully ascertain this type of horrific, life-changing information as part of a normal conversation. Brain damage? What does this mean? The questions spew uncontrollably from my thoughts. Does this mean Carol will survive? Will she survive but have brain damage? How much brain damage? Can she still have a quality of life? No quality of life? I instinctively think I can take care of her and provide her with everything she would need. Then another series of thoughts... oh my God, what if she can't speak or move? What if her quality of life is compromised to such a degree that she can't have any sort of happy, functional life? All these questions race through my mind at the *same* time. This is so unfair, Carol is so not deserving of this. Panic is standing next to me and I refuse to acknowledge it or give it power.

The doctor tells me the next forty-eight hours are pivotal and will reveal what direction she/we are heading. He leaves and we are collectively stunned. I look at Linda and we both share a sense of remorse and silent recognition. I can see the shock and fear in both Chris and Melissa's faces, trying to comprehend this sudden reality that just dropped into all our lives.

I ask Kenny to give me a sense of what happened when he arrived at the house. He tells me when he and Linda arrived the police officers would not allow them to go inside the house. I think to myself, "Police officers?" He tells me the paramedics were working on Carol for twenty minutes to a half-hour inside the house. I begin trying to figure out the time frame in relationship to when Carol's heart stopped twice. If her heart stopped twice during those twenty-minutes at the house, one would logically assume they took place approximately ten minutes apart. Would those ten minutes be under the time frame that would cause brain damage? Too many questions, too many thoughts, too few answers.

I arrive back home that evening and see three packages in front of the door. A sense of profound sadness engulfs me. I would often tease Carol and tell her, "Every day when I come home, I see packages at the door or just inside the house. I wonder what she ordered this time. Is this going to be her last order?

I walk in the door and see a pair of Carol's blue shoes placed on one of the steps leading upstairs. When did she place them there? I momentarily think, "Will she wear those shoes again?" I fight to get these thoughts out of my head.

I bring the packages in the kitchen and see an egg-and-cheese on a roll lying on the island. It is still in the package it was delivered in with only a few bites taken out of the sandwich. Was it then, after that second bite, that Carol started feeling something was seriously wrong? I take the sandwich and toss it in the garbage. I take a deep breath and begin opening the packages. The first package is a pair of cotton pajamas from Victoria's Secret. The second package is a black sweater. The third is a sign that reads, *PETROSINOS, established in 2018.* This is similar to a sign we received from our friend Isabelle as a gift for our East Quogue home when we bought the house in 2015. Carol bought this for our new home, a home in which we were planning to spend the rest of our lives creating new memories. This is just life being unnecessarily cruel. If I was writing a scene and included this last package, that last sign, most people would say it's over the top and not believable. I swear I am in a script I have no control over, a story I can't re-write. We are just beginning the start of our new life in this beautiful house. We are supposed to be hosting our grandchildren's birthday parties, celebrating anniversaries, hosting holidays, growing old here.

I look at the sign and the potential of where we are heading and it's just too emotionally and psychologically overwhelming, so unfair, so devastating. I am held captive by this pain and the reality it presents. Without warning, in this private horrific moment, my body and emotions submit to this heartbreak, and I am emotionally overwhelmed.

I gather myself, pour a glass of red wine, and walk outside to our backyard. I sit down and slowly sip the wine. I feel a brief moment of sereneness, of normalcy, and I embrace it like a lover's hug. I never thought I would appreciate normalcy as much I do in this briefest of moments.

I reflect on the first time Carol and I walked back here while being given a tour of the house. We looked at each other and simply smiled. She knew my idea of a hidden oasis is escaping to the backyard to either read the morning paper, get lost in a good book, or simply sit with her and share a quiet dinner. As we walked back inside the house that day, she turned and said, "*You're going to love staying in that back-yard.*"

Now, as I sit here alone, I wonder, "*Will we ever have a quiet dinner together back here again?*" I take my time and use the serenity of the moment to once again organize my thoughts. I want to gather some clarity as to where Carol is as well as where I am. One of my favorite sayings is "*Clarity at all costs,*" although the costs have never been so high as they are now.

I sit in the backyard until it turns dark, a hundred thoughts rushing through my head, very few holding on for more than a few seconds. I try to comprehend this new reality I seem to be heading for and what it may mean. Will Carol survive this? If she does, will she have brain damage? How much brain damage? What will I need to do to help her?

I visualize the moments we have shared during the short time we have been in the new house. Danielle teaching Aiden how to swim and holding Aubrey-Lynn at the same time; Chris placing Anthony in a float and Anthony laughing loudly; the barbecue with my friend Cathy and her family after not seeing them for nearly thirty years. Just *two* days ago we celebrated Labor Day weekend! I remember how happy and blessed we felt to see our children and grandchildren enjoying our new home. I reminisce about the moments Carol and I had simply drinking wine and talking. Is it going to end so quickly now? We are just beginning this stage in our lives, looking forward to this new adventure. I stop myself from having these negative thoughts. Am I over-reacting or simply being logical? Am I preparing myself for what I fear is coming, or what I know is coming, the worst-case scenario?

I first encountered the pain of losing someone significant in my life when I was twenty-one and my seventeen-year-old brother Frank (affectionately known as Cheech), was killed in a motorcycle accident. I was introduced to the overwhelming pain, questions, anger, and shock that seem to be part of the human process of coping with grief at that level of loss. Those feelings surround me once again like a shark circling its prey and I'm fighting to keep them away. Carol is still alive, and she will be OK. She has to be.

That night I go into the bedroom and Carol is not there. I wonder if she will ever lie with me again in this bed as husband and wife. I walk throughout the room and instinctively stare at her jewelry and recall how good it looked on her. I look at where she placed each piece of jewelry and imagine her placing them in those exact spots. I wonder if she will ever wear them again. Have to get these thoughts out of my head.

I lie in the bed and keep myself from looking over at the empty space where Carol sleeps. That night, I have a dream about Carol. I truly believe it was a visit from her. I am standing in an alley and see Carol about ten yards away standing beside an Uber car. I ask her not to go into the car. She smiles a gentle, sad smile, waves goodbye, enters the car, and it pulls away.

I know people will say the dream is simply a reflection of my own subconscious mind about the events of the day, what is happening to me at that moment, and my own worst fears; and perhaps they would be right, but in my heart, I *know* it is Carol telling me, preparing me for, how this is going to end. I wake up knowing she won't be returning to us.

## Two Weeks at the Hospital

The next two weeks at Robert Wood Johnson Hospital, waiting to see if Carol is going to wake up from her coma, are the worst two weeks of my life. I still see vignettes throughout that horrible time. I remember sharing my dream of Carol with my son's father-in-law, Larry, and telling him I didn't have a good feeling about how this was going to end. I feel I am in a battle that pits my anticipation of a tragic ending, especially given the dream I had, against Danielle and Chris's hope and their positive and reassuring spirit that Carol will be all right. They present different scenarios for a positive ending, even including ideas about how we will work together to deal with any kind of brain damage Carol might have. I am so proud of the people they have become. In my private moments with Carol during this time at the hospital, I often share thoughts about what a good job we did raising them and how individually strong they both are. As they share their hope, I find myself almost feeling guilty knowing something they don't. Mom is not coming back. I catch myself from continuing to think negatively.

The first few days at the hospital, the focus is on waiting for Carol to open her eyes. Every breath, every sound of an alarm from one of the pieces of apparatus that surround her, is met with hopeful anticipation and wishful prayers. I painfully watch Danielle, Chris, other family members and friends speak so lovingly to Carol. I am moved by their love, their encouraging words to her, and their absolute hope of recovery. We sit, stand, walk, talk, and continue waiting over hours and days for that moment when she will open her eyes, waiting for *any* sign of improvement, movement, life. I feel the time waiting at the hospital is becoming more about preparing us for the finality to come.

During this time, I am a consumed with finding out exactly what was taking place during the course of the morning of Carol's heart attack. What was she emotionally, psychologically, and physically going through?

How did this escalate so quickly? What did we miss? I miss? I go back over my text messages and Carol's from that morning to try to get a better understanding of the step-by-step course of what transpired and what she was experiencing.

After I left to go to work that morning, the first text message Carol sent was to Danielle around 7:00 a.m. She then called me at 7:20 a.m., while I was on the train, to tell me she spoke with Danielle and told her she wasn't going to be able to babysit. I thought her panic attack must be severe for her to cancel babysitting for both Danielle and Melissa. We spoke briefly and she said she would call me back, which she did at 7:35 a.m. to tell me she was feeling anxious and wished I was there with her. She texted Danielle at 7:40 a.m. and me again at 7:50 a.m. just to say she wanted to talk, which we did for a short time until she said she had to go. How vulnerable and afraid she must have felt. When we were dating after her mom had passed, Carol would call me at night just wanting to talk. Often, she would fall asleep while we were on the phone. She just wanted to connect which she was doing again that morning.

She never explained to me that she was feeling something different, never mentioned anything about her heart. I have to believe, she thought this was also a panic attack and wasn't aware it was actually a heart attack until later that morning.

Her next call was to Linda at 11:13 a.m. telling her she wasn't feeling good and that she missed Carroll Street and her mother. When Linda shared with me that Carol, "*missed her mother*," that alarmed me even more. She told Linda she loved her, and needed to "*call my husband*" and said goodbye. I believe it was at this time, Carol started to recognize that what she was experiencing was not a panic attack, but a heart attack. She was approaching panic mode.

Hearing Linda tell me Carol missed Carroll Street makes me sad and confused at the same time. Sad because Carol she said she missed the old neighborhood and confused because Carol and I were adamant in our agreement that it was time to move out of Brooklyn. During a year of house hunting, Carol would always return excited about the homes she saw. She would often say she wanted to move out of the neighborhood because it wasn't the neighborhood she remembered growing up.

When we first visited the Manalapan house, we hadn't walked ten feet into the house when Carol was jumping up and down and we looked at each other knowing this was *the* house. When we moved in, we would often eat outside in the backyard. I can still see and hear Carol pausing while having dinner, looking at the trees on a beautiful summer evening, saying, *"It's so serene here."* I remember feeling happy that she was happy and having that serenity.

Throughout the two weeks, the reports are consistently not favorable. Every night when I return home, there are packages waiting for me outside the door and then during the last few days, the packages stop arriving. My alone time with Carol at the hospital, is often holding her hand, looking at her hands and asking myself if this is going to be the final day when I can actually touch her. She had beautiful hands. I would periodically tell her she should have been a hand model. Seeing her hands so swollen yet still beautiful is another painful visual memory.

After the first week, the doctors take Carol off the thermo blanket and her body temperature begins to climb. She has still not awakened, and I recall feeling that, we are reaching the beginning of the end of this horrific time at the hospital.

At the end of that first week, my mindset changes. I end each day sitting in my backyard, alone, thinking, planning what to do next. I reluctantly start thinking about funeral plans. Should Carol be buried with her parents at Holy Cross Cemetery or should I purchase more plots and have her buried with me and my family? Should I cremate her as she once mentioned or was she just being humorous? Thoughts I am not prepared for, decisions I am not ready to make.

Every night during those two weeks, when I go to bed, I purposely stay on my side of the bed without turning or looking toward where Carol slept. To think she will no longer be sleeping with me, lying on my chest, brings a profound sadness. The realization is heartbreaking and impossible to share.

When someone asks how I am feeling, I often say the same line: "*I feel like I've just been shot in the stomach with a bazooka.*" I look down at the hole in my body and I ask myself, "*What now?*"

In Joan Didion's excellent book; *The Year of Magical Thinking*, she shares a story about her own experience dealing with the process of grieving for her husband and then her daughter. Throughout the book, Ms. Didion periodically returns to the thought, "*You sit down to dinner and life as you know it ends.*" That phrase deeply resonates with me and I think, "*I go to work and life as I know it ends.*"

During this time, I have another dream of Carol and, once again, I have no doubt it was another visit. One of the major pains for me is the loss of the beautiful relationship between Carol and Danielle's son, Aiden, our oldest grandchild. Carol babysat for Aiden three days a week and they developed a special bond that was beautiful to observe. He referred to her as Gigi. There are countless pictures of Carol with Aiden: holding him, reading to him, hugging and laughing with him. The expression on her face in each and every picture is so loving. To think that relationship is ending so soon, and that our younger grandchildren are not getting an opportunity to know and experience Carol, is a major trigger for me. It simply is unfair, gut wrenching, and is the only time I feel any real sense of anger. Not at God, or Carol, just at the reality of this situation. It is so final.

One of the major thoughts that bothers me is whether Carol is going to be at peace given that she will not be with her grandchildren and watch them grow up. No longer having that special relationship with Aiden who she had the most time to bond with.

That night I have a dream I am holding Aiden in the kitchen of my daughter's former apartment when Carol walks in. At first, the dream feels so real that I actually experience what it would feel like if Carol awakened from her coma. I am shocked and thrilled to see her walking into the kitchen, dressed in her blue hospital gown. She continues walking peacefully into the kitchen and passes me and Aiden without saying a word or making eye contact. By the end of the dream, knowing I am beginning to wake up, I fight hard to stay in the dream but to no avail. I wake up and immediately sense this is Carol's way of telling me not to be concerned about this, because she will not be losing that love with Aiden and her grandchildren but experiencing it in a different and much more profound way. I also come away feeling she wants me to be more proactive in our grandchildren's lives.

Again, people can logically say I am only fooling myself, and believing what I "want" or "need" to believe. But in my heart, I know this was a true encounter, a real message, and the clarity overwhelmingly resonates with me.

Carol had a profound love for all her grandchildren. I remember Carol and I having to wait three months to move into our new home and staying with Chris and Melissa, during that time. It was a blessing because Melissa gave birth to Anthony while we were living with them. Late one night, Anthony began crying and Carol quickly jumped out of bed and went to him, not wanting an exhausted Melissa to get up. I still see Carol gently cradling Anthony in her arms and smiling so lovingly at him. After he went back to sleep, I asked her to come back to bed but instead she continued holding him and told me she was going to stay with him a bit longer.

It is heartbreaking that my grandchildren will no longer experience the love Carol had for them. What will Anthony or any of my grandchildren know about Carol? We as a family will certainly share our stories and pictures and let them know what a special woman she was, and how much "Gigi" loved them. For me, this is personally one of the most difficult and emotional challenges to overcome.

After the first week, just before the weekend, Carol's doctor tells me we are not heading down the course we want and that I should start to prepare the family and get "things" in order. I ask the doctor what the standard timeframe is before he can one-hundred-percent say Carol will not be opening her eyes again. He tells me that although the current data supports his prognosis, if I want to fully extend the time limit, they will give it another week. But he emphasizes that a different, more favorable outcome isn't likely. He also presents me the option of moving Carol to a different facility where she would be fed by a tube and asks if I want to keep her on life support. Carol and I had discussed this issue a few times over the years and we both promised each other we would never allow that to happen to either one of us. I choose to extend her stay another week but not to have her placed on life support.

During the last week at Robert Wood Johnson Hospital, I see the best and worst in people. Most of the nurses who take care of Carol during this time aren't just outstanding professionals, they are outstanding human beings who have genuine empathy and understanding about the importance of the human connection. I am grateful for their service, humanity and compassion during this challenging time.

Of course, there are always individuals who strictly see their job as a paycheck and, although unfortunate, I do understand their perspective. Their work in this wing has them surrounded by death and sadness every-day of their lives. I would think there is a primal defense mechanism not to get personally caught up in the lives of their patients or their families during this time. I see this as simply psychological survival. However, there is one neurologist who angers both Danielle and me. He enters the room and begins a series of tests to determine if Carol has any neurological functions. After performing the tests, as if he is working on a car, he methodically approaches me and Danielle and, in a matter-of-fact way, reads us the findings like a math teacher reading the answer to an equation. He tells us given Carol's condition and test results, almost ninety-five percent of the patients with these numbers don't make it. Before we have a chance to respond, he asks if we have any questions. My gut response is to say, "Yes, when did you become such an insensitive asshole?"

I certainly understand that a doctor has an obligation to share factual information no matter how bad and painful the news is to the patient's family members. I also understand a doctor has no stake in the results. Saying that, doctors should at least present a sense of empathy and *respect* when communicating horrific life-changing information knowing the information they are sharing not only destroys the one-thing families in these situations are grasping onto- hope-but also the person you are sharing that information with.

After that meeting, I start leaving the hospital a little earlier. I arrive early in the morning and stay till around 5:00 p.m., feeling exhausted in every way a human being can, knowing the outcome. I have countless conversations with Carol during this time, balancing between trying to keep her hopeful in case she can hear me and letting her know how blessed I am for her presence in my life and for her love and loyalty during the thirty-eight years we journeyed together as husband and wife. I tell her how much I love her countless times and how much I will always love her, how grateful I am that our love produced two amazing children, grandchildren, and I ask her to guide and teach me how to move forward without her. Every night I ask God to guide me to the right choices and to give me the strength, courage, and wisdom to make them. I now have Carol helping me as well.

I know the last few days at the hospital are serving to transition from the reality we shared for forty-three years together to a new uncharted reality. Preparing for the end of life as I know it with Carol. How do I do this? The finality of Carol's passing is incomprehensible and I am at a loss for words to describe the pain and sadness I feel.

The doctors tell me they are going to take Carol off life support the afternoon of September 19 and I am given a sense of what that process is going to be like. The finality of this moment defeats hope, opening the door to every negative emotion and fear you have been fighting desperately to keep away. It is a moment that is overwhelming and the pain and sadness not comprehensible. As the doctors leave, I remain standing there, my body numb, my heart broken and my mind struggling to grasp it all. I tell my children I will be at her side till the end.

For the next three days, I watch as, one by one, family and friends come to say their last goodbyes. I see and agonize watching from afar, what seems surreal, each one speaking to Carol in hushed, reverent tones, tears in their eyes; each one having their own private confession with her. I watch painfully through the window from outside the room as Chris and Danielle say their final goodbyes to the mother who bore them, guided them, and loved them unconditionally.

How can this truly be happening? How? And *why* is this happening? I watch my daughter's eyes, her expression of disbelief, staring at her mother in a way I have never seen before, talking to her quietly, reverently and then quickly leaving the room and the hospital. I feel the pain watching my Chris fight to stay strong, his tears falling on the sheet, whispering in his mother's ear, the sadness in his eyes betraying his strength.

When all are gone, at 12:54 in the afternoon, the equipment that is keeping her alive is removed and the clock begins ticking. My thoughts and conversation with Carol change during the course of our final moments together. When will she pass? What will be my last words to her? I remind her of all the good in our lives, her legacy and all the blessings in our life together. I tell her again how much I love her and promise to be close to our children and grandchildren and take care of them as she always did. I tell her what is happening to her and that there should be no regrets. I hold her face and tell her she will be seeing her mother, father, and Marietta soon and to send my love to them and my brother and father. I tell her to let go and go to the light.

At around 11:30 p.m., sitting by Carol's side, I fall asleep. At 12:52 a.m., I suddenly feel a tremendous ice-cold sensation over my entire body, as if someone has put my body in a deep freezer. I wonder what is happening to me before I even wake up. As I begin to open my eyes and spring up from the chair, the cold sensation leaves me and in the very next instant, Carol's alarm goes off. I immediately realize Carol has given me a great gift. I know she touched me, wanting to let me know she was leaving this earth and was at peace, before the alarm woke me. The nurse enters the room and confirms Carol has passed but I already know from Carol's gift, when she said goodbye and let me know she was OK, that she was moving on and at peace. I will always cherish and be grateful for that moment for that was truly Carol.

I leave the hospital at 1:30 a.m., and enter an Uber I called for. I sit numb and, in this moment, defeated, and isolated in the introductory stage of this horrible new reality without Carol. The driver tries to be engaging and start a conversation. He is upbeat, perhaps too upbeat given the time and certainly the place I am in. He asks me why I was at the hospital and when I tell him, the rest of the ride passes in silence.

I arrive home around two in the morning, and the house immediately feels emptier than ever. I don't want to be here, alone, without Carol. Our dog Chloe, greets me and is the only hint of a normalcy that no longer exists here. I call my family one by one, a call each is expecting, and officially share the tragic news. The rest of the early morning is also an official introduction to the reality of grief, the pain it holds, and the battle that lies ahead.

*"I go to work and life as I know it ends"*.

## The Wake

Merriam –Webster's Dictionary defines grief as (a) *A deep and poignant distress caused by or as if by bereavement*, (b) *a cause of such suffering*, (c) *an unfortunate outcome: disaster*. Yes…disaster.

I believe there is no more dreaded and painful emotion human beings face than grief. The pain of grief, mourning the loss of someone you love, is probably the most devastating and challenging battle we all will confront. Yet grief, this most worthy challenger to humanity, also brings out the most humanity in people.

During this terrible time of my life, I have seen acts of humanity not only from family and close friends, but from people I don't have direct day-to-day contact with. I have encountered neighbors, students and former students, colleagues, and, in some cases, total strangers who genuinely and sincerely embraced me with a profound caring and respect, almost in a reverent way, sometimes holding back their own emotions, and sometimes not. Grief makes us all vulnerable, to those experiencing it, and those who are around it. Grief forces you to encounter your worst fears, it takes you to your weakest places and dares you to test whether or not you have it in you to fight it. Yet, grief also lets you see the best of yourself, what you truly are capable of and the humanity in others.

I have learned that as painful as grief is, a *disaster*, grief also brings out the best in our humanity and brings people together. I haven't stopped to analyze why, I will leave that to the psychologists and therapists. I can only think that it's the one true primal emotion we *all* fear, can relate to, and have empathy for. We grasp the absolute finality of it, the magnitude of what it does to the core of us, the damaging effects, and we respond in our most primal and human capacity to try to overcome it or feel empathy toward those who are going through it. No matter our backgrounds, religious beliefs, or political differences, grief universally connects us.

The number of people at Carol's wake is a moving testament to the love and respect people have for her. My colleagues and friends at the School of Visual Arts, some of whom I haven't seen in many years, move and humble me by attending and make me appreciate each of them even more. As I say to Danielle and Chris, the overflow of people attending Carol's wake should remind us how blessed we are to have so many wonderful people in our lives who love and respect us as well.

The Church service at Sacred Hearts Saint Stephen in Carroll Gardens, Brooklyn, is a surreal experience. I feel like this is a rehearsal for a scene in a movie but the pain lets me know this is very real. I stand inside the entrance of the church and the funeral director indicates when to enter and where to go according to a traditional Catholic funeral mass. Chris is one of the pallbearers along with Linda and Kenny's oldest son, Kenny Jr., whom we have known since he was a young boy. As I start walking down the center of the aisle, I glance over to the pew where Carol and I regularly sat just about every Sunday for 10:00 a.m. mass. For so many years, we would sit in the second pew in the middle of the church on the left, me always on the aisle seat. Yet this time, although we enter the church together, we pass our spot and separate. Reverend Monsignor Guy Massie, the pastor of Sacred Hearts & Saint Stephen Church, presides over the mass, which makes me happy, as he is a friend to our family. The church is filled, and Monsignor Massie presents a loving heart-warming tribute to Carol.

Danielle speaks and presents a beautiful homage to her mother. She decides not to write anything down and simply speaks from her heart. I follow and read from my notes. At first, I was simply going to place what I wrote in the casket with Carol but decide I want to honor her and let people know not only how much I love her, but how I personally feel about Carol the human being.

I look at my notes and periodically pause as I read the words. It's amazing how your body takes control and let's you know your emotions need to pause. You have absolutely no control over this. It's not just about the emotional aspect, it's also about the truth of what I'm saying. I fight through and finish speaking.

When the mass concludes, the funeral director guides me to walk behind the casket and head toward the rear of the church. I take a moment to pause where Carol and I sat and one last time, I visualize the two of us sitting at our spot.

After thanking each person individually who attended the service, we enter the limousine. The plan is to stay with tradition and have the hearse pass by our former home on Carroll Street for one last goodbye. As we are about to make the turn onto the block, we see that an ambulance is double-parked down the street preventing cars from entering. Cars are backing up and we cannot enter the block to pass the house.

I wonder if this is a coincidence or if there is some sort of symbolism here. Is it not good to look back? Should we keep our eyes looking toward the horizon? Does Carol NOT want to go back or does the house not want us back? Probably just a coincidence but nonetheless I find the timing ... interesting.

We head to Holy Cross Cemetery, the final stop of this procession. The finality of this moment is just too painful and surreal to fully explain. The day is sunny but brisk. A number of cars line up and we all approach the gravesite. While standing waiting for the priest to begin, I look at the headstone and remember Carol once telling me, when we visited this grave site to place a wreath for her mother during a Christmas holiday, that whenever one visits it's important to place a stone on the headstone to let the person know they were visited.

A priest I don't know begins speaking and I feel like I am in a nightmare. No one is in focus, voices are muted, and I am lost in too many thoughts, too many emotions. The priest concludes his prayers and we each place a rose on the casket. When I place my rose on the casket, I recall the time my father was so devastated by the death of my brother, that he could barely toss his rose.

The casket begins being lowered but they have problems lowering it. I mistakenly wait too long for the casket to be lowered but decide to leave. Others follow.

We leave as a group, hug each other, say our muted respectful good-byes, and soon arrive at my son's home in Matawan, where we follow tradition and have immediate family and friends gather to eat and to support each other. I remember standing outside and telling my cousin Frank, *"I can't wait till this day is over so I will never have to say, "I buried my wife today."* I don't expect a response, what can anyone say to that? I don't get one.

When everyone leaves, I take Chloe, for a long walk. I think I need the walk more than she does. I find myself in front of a senior citizens home and walk through the parking area. Toward the back of the community there is a playground and a bench that overlooks a quiet, wooded area. I sit alone on the bench and try to comprehend the day, the events, and perhaps, in some way, myself and what is in front of me. It's not possible as I am emotionally and psychologically on autopilot. Somehow, I find an unexpected calm, an unexpected serenity here. I privately submit to the emotions I have held back all day.

*"I go to work and life as I know it ends."*


## Coming Back Home

The first few weeks after Carol's passing are an array of daily emotional and psychological challenges, plus reality checks I don't expect. Going back to the house without her presence, and she was and still is such a strong presence, is excruciating. She is everywhere, from the design of the house, to the furniture, plants, and knick-knacks, to the food in the refrigerator and pantry, to the pots and pans in the kitchen. Yet, she is nowhere. Every aspect of the house, every moment, has suddenly turned into a memory now. Although it's heartbreaking and sad being alone in the house, I have a strong connection to Carol here. This is the home *we* loved, shared, and spent too short a time in together.

The first time being alone in the house, I look at the items in the pantry and in some strange way, don't want to touch or use them since Carol placed them there. Isn't this a crazy thought? Is this just me at my most vulnerable and weakest moment?

In the refrigerator there is baby food, kid drinks, and snacks that Carol stocked for when she would babysit our grandchildren. I pack it all up and give it to Danielle and Melissa. I don't need an additional reminder of the life I have suddenly lost and of not having Aiden, Aubrey and Anthony here just about every day.

Nighttime is the absolute worst. The silence of the house is palpable a bully waiting for me. Thank God for Chloe. She is a friend and a companion who follows me from room to room and lies next to me. Her presence is comforting and a thread of normalcy. Chloe was at the house when Carol had her heart attack and I sometimes look at Chloe and wonder what she saw that morning as the events unfolded. If only she could communicate.

I go upstairs to the bedroom and it is one of the hardest things I have ever had to do, the *harshest* reality check in the finality of this. My eyes immediately focus on our wedding picture that sits on the table near Carol's side of the bed, both of us smiling, hopeful about the beginning of our lives together as husband and wife, and it is absolutely heartbreaking.

I enter her walk-in closet. I don't know why. I see her shoes, clothes, sweaters, and pocketbooks as she last left them, and it is gut-wrenching. Our master bathroom remains pretty much as it was that day, September 5. Carol's hair is still on the brush, her soaps, cleansers, and moisturizers placed exactly where she last left them. This is too painful, and I ask myself,

"Why am I doing this?" Is this also a natural part of the grieving process or is it just me, lost in my own head?

Trying to fall asleep in our bed, alone, is the biggest emotional and psychological test and one of the worst moments. I wouldn't wish it on my worst enemy. I find that if I sleep with my back turned away from where Carol slept, I will not have to look across to an empty side of the bed where she would, should be. I turn on the television, put the volume on low, and hold the remote in my hand. When I find myself falling asleep, I shut the TV off and fall asleep with the remote in my hand.

Another reality check: I have never lived alone. I went from living with my parents, to being married to Carol and moving into her Brooklyn home. I'm not used to all the quiet, the down time, and the lack of conversation, companionship, activity, discussions, and yes, even the arguments in the house. This takes me by surprise. I wasn't anticipating that my reaction to living alone is something else I will have to adjust to. Another form of emptiness I wasn't expecting.

I reflect on how active the house always was. Coming home from work and looking forward to seeing my grandchildren waiting for me. Often times Danielle staying for dinner and my son-in law Chris D, joining us. Now, when I sit in the kitchen to have dinner, the stillness lingers almost to the point of engulfing me. Toys are still in the family room closet and inside the toy chest leading to the basement. I don't want to look at all this but how can I avoid it? *Should* I avoid it? I think about Aiden, Aubrey, and Anthony running through this now silent house. We will have to come up with a plan and find a babysitting solution. I know I will most likely be involved in some way now.

Yet another new experience is presented that I will have to adjust to; I have always disliked eating alone. Carol and I routinely ate together ever since we were married and especially when Danielle and Chris were growing up. When they grew older and married, we would still eat together at the house or go out to dinner. When I eat at home now, I look at the empty chair next to me and my stomach churns.

When we moved to New Jersey, we ate out often, maybe three times a week. We were exploring our new surroundings together. I think in some ways I felt most close to Carol during this time. We were sharing a new adventure together and going out to eat provided us an opportunity, an intimacy perhaps, that allowed us to be together, talk, and share this new chapter in our lives, a real quality time.

To break the routine of being alone, I alternate sleeping at Danielle's home, Chris's home, and my own home. I am grateful and blessed to have children who love me and genuinely want me to stay with them. If there are two shining examples of the best of what Carol and I accomplished together, it is by far the two of them. I give Carol a lot of credit for setting up their foundations and giving them love, guidance, and support, but I also applaud them for the work they have done on themselves. They are strong individuals who are fighting through their own grief and pain. They validate the adage *"Love conquers all."* Their love, generosity, and tremendous hearts, have taught me to be more thankful for them and to my extended family and friends who genuinely and unconditionally love and support us. It is the combination of my faith, the integrity of my life, and the love of the people around me that allows me to continue having a desire to move forward and to even be open to exploring the new journey ahead. I just find it hard to believe I have become a nomad.

When we sold the house on Carroll Street, we couldn't immediately move into our new home in Manalapan so Carol and I stayed with Danielle and Chris D for a week, sleeping on an air mattress in the living room. Then when Chris and Melissa moved into their new home, Carol and I stayed with them and graduated to having our own room, a closet, and a drawer! Now I'm back to that life style on a part-time basis.

Carol took care of all our finances. From managing the bills to buying groceries, she was the point person. She created all the on-line passwords, placed all the orders, and made all the payments. Now, without any preparation or window of opportunity to learn, I find myself unexpectedly having to become that point person, on the fly. Carol, spoiled me, protected me from dealing with paying the bills and now I have to learn *quickly*.

I need to make a plan and my first step is to identify the companies Carol has been paying and locate as many passwords as possible for each account. I start by reviewing emails Carol had on her cellphone from the businesses and credit card companies she was dealing with. I go through her bag, which alone is emotionally difficult, and take out all the credit cards. I separate the credit cards that are solely in Carol's name, and those that are in both of our names. I spent two days calling credit card companies. I remove a significant amount of the credit cards solely by closing out the accounts that were under Carol's name and pay off the balances on the other cards. Within a short amount of time, and with guidance from Melissa's father, Larry, I begin to get a grasp of the total picture and we develop a game plan to pay all of them in full.

I imagine there are people like me who also lost their spouse and suddenly find themselves in an unfamiliar situation of having to take over the financial responsibilities of the house; trying to identify *who* are the companies you owe money to, *what* are the amounts due, *where* are the passwords, and perhaps *why* these bills even exist. I suddenly find myself in a difficult and uncomfortable situation that I wasn't prepared for. Larry was a blessing who helped me through a difficult situation and I am forever grateful for his patience and guidance.

I have spoken with several married couples since and it seems I am not alone in this. A number of them shared that one or the other is *solely* responsible for paying the bills and managing the finances while the other knows little about it. They confided that my experience has made them realize *both* partners need to be involved.

Danielle has also been amazing putting together a chart of companies, as well as setting up on-line payments, passwords, and due dates, which has given me a sense of clarity and control managing the finances.

When we sold our house on Carroll Street, we did it through a 1031 Exchange, which required us to re-invest the money we received from the sale of the house into other real estate properties. Part of this investment was used to purchase two townhouses in Pembroke Pines, Florida, as rental properties. Melissa has been tremendous helping me manage the properties, making sure my HOA and mortgage payment on one of the houses are paid on time. I have come to realize how time consuming this is and how much one really has to constantly be on top of things.

I ask myself, where I was in all this? What was my responsibility? Why wasn't I more aware of the finances? Did I simply fall into the conventional trap of feeling comfortable with my wife handling the finances? Carol had been handling the bills since we were married so it was sort of a natural fit that she continued till the day she passed.

## October 17

Today is Carol's birthday and our anniversary. We would have been married thirty-eight years today. As I write that line, I am forced to pause as it is surreal to change the words from *have been* married to *would have been* married. In less than a month, not only have the words changed, but so too my world. I have gone from *married* to *widowed* to *single*, in the blink of an eye.

I am going to the cemetery today for the first time since the burial. I don't want anyone with me as I anticipate this will be an emotional day and wouldn't want to put anyone in that uncomfortable situation. Plus, I need my alone time with Carol.

I head to Holy Cross Cemetery not fully sure how to get to the gravesite. I enter the front gates and after a few turns, I am officially lost. Another analogy? I go to the main office inside the cemetery and they give me a map and direct me.

I drive and within minutes I am in the area of the gravesite and it all looks familiar, too familiar. I stay in the car and see the rerun of her burial in my mind. I remember the line of cars that stood here less than a month ago only this time I am alone and the weather is chilly and cloudy. I already start feeling emotionally overwhelmed. I don't know if it's even worth fighting it and decide just to move forward.

I step out of the car and see the head stone, which is about twenty-five yards from me, the recently dug up dirt still fresh and visible. As I walk toward the grave, I feel the weight of this moment with every step I take. I am not only aware of the melancholy that is rapidly engulfing me and taking control, but also the physical reaction as my muscles tighten and my heart starts to race. I am instinctively reacting to the reality of this moment and have absolutely no control. It is *horrific*.

The nearly one month since Carol's passing finds me standing over her gravesite, officially *confronting* the tragic finality of it all. It is intimate, personal, and heart-wrenching. I arrive at the gravesite and firmly place the roses and their stand deep into the ground. Carol always loved roses and she would let me know whenever I forgot or bought different flowers. I don't want to disappoint her.

I stand up and before I can finish wishing Carol a happy birthday and anniversary, I find myself sobbing like a child. I thank her for our life together, for Danielle and Chris and for her love and devotion. I tell her I will stay strong, will be proactive in our children's and grandchildren's lives, and ask her for guidance. The sorrow and pain of this moment is overwhelming. I am against the ropes, getting pummeled and fighting to simply find an opportunity to pause, even for a moment. Before leaving, I ask Carol to watch over us.

When I return home, I feel emotionally, physically, and psychologically drained. I pour myself a glass of wine, reflect on the day and ask myself, what's next. How do I move forward from here without her? Today is one of the saddest days in my life and the genesis of this journal.

I have never written a journal before, didn't feel a need to, but after going through the pain and sadness of today, with so many confusing thoughts and painful emotions going through me at the same time, I don't want to go through this time in my life in a pedestrian way. I want to go deeper, to better understand what I am encountering, and my response to each encounter. I want to be able to pull back the covers and understand my place in all this and, perhaps, understand myself better. I also want to leave a legacy for Danielle, Chris, and my grandchildren. I want Aiden, Aubrey, Anthony, and any other future grandchildren, to know who Carol was, and how much she loved them.

## October 21

I have another dream about Carol. She wants to separate; I tell her I don't want us to part. She says I will be OK, and wishes me luck with my friends. I'm not sure if she is referring to future friends, or people I know. I believe she means friends I know. I tell her the best times in my life will always be the ones we shared together. She pauses for the briefest of moments revealing just a hint of sadness, and leaves. I wake up and think about this dream long into the night.

# Thanksgiving

I sleep at Danielle's because I don't want to wake up alone on Thanksgiving morning in my house. Danielle and I spend a good amount of time in the morning talking about Carol. Although the initial shock has passed, the wound is fresh and the reality of Carol's absence lingers heavily with all of us. Danielle thinks I should go to therapy but what can a therapist tell me that I don't already know or feel? It may sound ignorant, but I understand the reality I'm confronted with. I walk a fine line wanting to speak to my children about Carol but I don't want be a trigger for them because I struggle to keep my emotions in place whenever I speak out loud about her. I realize I will eventually get to a better place but *where is that place?*

I leave Danielle's and arrive back home. The first thing I do is put the Thanksgiving Day parade on the TV. It gives me a sense of normalcy and tradition I want to keep alive. The smells of the holiday season are *not* permeating throughout the house. The winds outside are the only sounds echoing through the house. Carol and I are not discussing if the stuffing should be cooked inside the turkey or separately. Thanksgiving is a day to give thanks, putting another dual challenge in front of me. The thought of Carol not being here to share this day against the mindset of being thankful for my family and friends. I fight through the natural emotions that are inviting me to be sad and I fight to choose to be thankful and acknowledge my blessings. Thankful for Carol and her legacy I see around me. Thankful for the love of my children, grand children, extended family and for the life we shared. I *choose* not to linger in sadness. In my head, I maintain that ability to choose, but my heart has other ideas.

I arrive at Chris and Melissa's home with Chloe. Larry and Lisa are already there along with Melissa's sister Andrea, and her husband Frankie, as well as other members of Melissa's family. They are all great people who greet me warmly yet with a respectful trepidation. I know my presence makes them feel Carol's absence even more. I have become the elephant in the room, a reminder of something tragic that makes them sad. Danielle arrives a bit later with Chris D, Aiden and Aubrey and we go on with the day.

Chris places a small picture of Carol along with a glass of wine next to it on the kitchen counter. My eyes automatically swell with tears, but I fight once again not to get emotional. This is going to be a constant battle today. The day goes by with subdued laughter, lighthearted jokes, and a lot of food. Sharing a meal always offers an important sense of community, as people gather, break bread and share an encounter together whether joyful or sad.

I find that as the day moves on, although I genuinely love everyone sharing this day, I need my own quiet time, so I take a walk with Chloe once again to the spot I favor whenever I visit my son's home, a playground at a nearby senior citizens development. I find my usual bench and sit gazing at the wide-open wooded area just opposite the large fence. It's a place that somehow, always gives me a sense of intimacy with Carol and allows me to take a breath, pause, and feel peaceful. It's cold and I watch the tall, narrow, leafless trees sway in the wind. I instantly connect with the trees, swaying against the forces yet still standing. I think to myself, "*I am being a bit cinematic here*", but the symbolism feels honest.

I return to Chris and Melissa's house, my silent conversation with Carol over, and find Chris deep-frying the turkey in his garage. He asks me how I'm doing, and we start a conversation. I value this opportunity to be alone and have a conversation with him because Chris keeps things to himself despite my encouragement to express himself more. This is the way he has always been no matter what the situation. He admits to having a few Grey Goose and tonics and begins to open up ever so slightly about missing his mother. It's good to hear him express himself so I am careful not to interrupt him. He shares that he thinks of Carol almost every minute of the day and can visualize her in his house. There are times when he pauses to get a hold of his emotions. I am happy he is allowing himself to be open and vulnerable. Confronting the pain is part of healing.

A short time later, we sit down for Thanksgiving dinner. I look at all the food and remember how good a cook Carol was. From the turkey, to her famous zucchini, pumpkin and pecan pies, to the stuffed artichokes. Oh, the stuffed artichokes were the best! I visualize her sitting with us, sitting next to me, but I can't do this for too long. I quickly ask myself a familiar question: Is this a normal reaction of someone grieving? Is it healthy? Unhealthy? Once again, so many questions with no answers.

Chris stands up at the dinner table and expresses what everyone is feeling, Carol's absence. He shares his feelings about his mother in such a strong and eloquent manner. He expresses how much he used to take these moments for granted and promises he won't do so ever again. Carol, still teaching lessons about love and family. I am proud of him, his strength to get through the toast, and his heart. He is honest and to the point. I remain silent. Collectively we fight through our emotions and tears, finish the toast, and continue Thanksgiving dinner.

What have I learned from this first Thanksgiving without Carol? That death can *never* defeat love. It can only limit your potential for so long before you continue to move forward, value the good in your life even more, and embrace what is ahead. We may be kicked to the ground, wounded, bruised and battered, but we remain resilient for the very reason we mourn the people that left us, they taught us love, nurtured us, and although they are no longer physically with us, their love never dies and is always with us.

What I learned a long time ago with the death of my brother Frank, still rings true: Never to take anyone for granted. Value and embrace every moment you have with them, for their presence is a gift that can be gone in an instant, but *never* the love they gave you. Thirty-nine years later, that truth still resonates.

# December 1

I was invited to dinner by my cousin Frank and his wife, Jenny. It's always good to see them. During those horrible two weeks at the hospital, waiting for Carol to come out of her coma, they visited often and I will always be thankful for their love and presence during that time.

My cousins Dawn and Michael, who I don't often see, are there as well along with Chris, Melissa and Anthony. Frank and I grew up together in Bensonhurst, Brooklyn, and share a lot of history and stories. He is a spiritual man and one of the few people I can have a genuine conversation with about God despite our different perspectives and spiritual mindsets. We also differ in our political beliefs but that's just another example of two people loving each other, differences and all.

Frank and Jenny ask me how I'm feeling. This is a question I obviously get asked a lot and to which I truly don't know how to respond. My reply is often, "*Depends when you ask me,*" which is true. I can feel OK and see the beginning of the healing process, then see a piece of Carol's jewelry or clothing and immediately get hit with a profound sadness. I feel like a surfer navigating through a tsunami during a storm. I am in uncharted waters here, simply trying to get through without falling off the board. I realize that, although I will always carry beautiful memories that Carol and I shared, I will also carry the scars of this storm with me for as long as I live.

Frank tells me about a dinner he is attending in a few weeks with some of the people we grew up with in Brooklyn. He rattles off the names and many of them I remember with a nostalgic fondness; others, not so much. So many of the people Frank and I grew up with are either dead, or stuck in 1974. He invites me to the dinner. I am curious but not motivated. I tell him I will get back to him.

My cousin Michael shows me a picture of Carol and me sitting together at my uncle's birthday gathering last year. Once again, I find myself fighting not to get emotional. It's unsettling how suddenly a picture of Carol can become an emotional trigger for me. Will I always have these triggers? Will this wound ever *completely* heal?

I decide to spend the night at Chris and Melissa's house. Melissa opens up a gift box her mother bought for Anthony for Christmas. Inside the box is a Christmas ornament called *Elf On the Shelf*. The same ornament Carol would place on our Christmas tree when we hung ornaments. Every Christmas, each of us, Carol, Danielle, Chris and I, would have our own individual ornament we would place on the tree. Is this a coincidence? To add to this coincidence, there is a short letter from the creator of the Elf on the Shelf that is part of the package. The creator signs her first name at the end of the letter. Yes, her name is Carol.

Am I that vulnerable to consistently take what might be simple coincidences to a different level? Or, is it possible this isn't a coincidence at all, but a way Carol is letting us know she is still close by?

So, what to make of this evening? The people you encounter in your life who have shared a part of your history, your personal journey, each one of them plays some role you may not be aware of in your story. Encounters have meaning, purpose and sometimes, great potential. Carol helped shape our story together as well as my own individual story. The people I grew up with in the old neighborhood also played a role. A lesser role of course, but nonetheless, they are a supporting cast that in some way has helped shape who I am. Tonight was a reminder not to take *any* of these encounters for granted and simply place them away in storage to dust off and share a memory. People you encounter have a purpose and a potential that shouldn't be ignored but explored if possible.

With regards to the Elf on the Shelf, I don't believe this was a coincidence. For me, it's a reminder that Carol remains close to us and although we don't see her, we can still feel her presence and love. Life can't be lived from a logical perspective all the time. There is so much we don't know; so much to learn, so much we miss if we are not open to believing there is something beyond our understanding, beyond us.

# December 2

Just before dinner with Chris, Melissa, and Anthony, I receive a phone call from an administrator at Robert Wood Johnson Hospital saying there are two pieces of Carol's jewelry still at the hospital. Given my mindset when we were last there, I never thought about asking if Carol was wearing jewelry at the time of her heart attack. Knowing Carol, I should have realized she would have been.

Chris and I jump in the car after dinner and drive to the hospital. I remember the stores I saw along the highway, every day during those two weeks of going back and forth from the hospital. Three months later, they are now unpleasant memories.

I start to think about the jewelry she was wearing at the time of her heart attack and realize it will be another sad and painful moment when I pick it up and see what she was wearing that morning.

We get to the hospital. Chris stays in the car and I walk in. I know the lobby layout and have an instant flashback of my time here. I approach the front desk, introduce myself, and an officer hands me a brown manila envelope. I sign a form and I'm out the door. I don't want to open the envelope and see the jewelry until I get home. The ride back is mixed with silence, unspoken sadness, and conversation about Carol. It is still so surreal, so hard to accept, and this just makes it harder.

We get to the house and open the envelope. Inside is Carol's cross on a chain and a bracelet. I instantly visualize Carol wearing the jewelry on the day of her heart attack and I am immediately *engulfed* in sadness. Every item of hers is a trigger. I fight not to replay that morning scene again in my mind and work hard to stay strong. I realize it's not a good thing to hold your emotions in but I don't want to become emotional in front of Chris and Melissa. I get by the moment and tell them I need to get my clothes ready for work tomorrow. I go into my room, close the door and allow myself to cry.

## December 5

It's been three months since Carol's heart attack. I find myself wanting to fast forward the calendar. They say, time heals all wounds and although I understand the logic of this, being healed seems so very far away. Healing, yes, changed, definitely. After the three months that have passed, I am at a different place. I am healing but I am not sure I want to do the things that distance me from Carol. Sometimes it's a choice between reflection and pain, or staying focused in the present and feeling...just *feeling*. It's easy to reflect, to linger in the memories, to look at the pictures. I sometimes ask if I'm fighting myself from experiencing the process of grief simply because I am fighting to be strong. The questions and challenges are equally redundant. I guess it's a part of our human nature to find a way to survive, the head vs. the heart. Am I ready to start moving forward? Do I *want* to move forward and leave behind the life I've known for forty-three years? Again, is this yet another stage of the grieving process?

So, what did I learn today? Well sometimes there are simply no lessons to learn, you just go through this painful and sad journey and see how you come out of it. At this moment, I am like the boxer who has just been punched in the face with a roundhouse right and falls to the floor, nearly knocked out. I stagger to get up. I am stunned trying to comprehend what just happened and struggling to get a sense of where I'm at. The ref is counting, 10…9…8, I fight against the pain and confusion and staggering, I stand up, 7…6…5, I take a deep breath and move forward to fight, 4…3…2… I hit back with everything I have and for a moment, the briefest of moments, it feels good just to stand.

## December 6

I remember a short film I once wrote and directed called *Moments*. It's a story about a young woman whose husband is killed in a war. The love they had was unique and profound. The question the film posed is: When you find someone who shows you that everything you thought about love is real, and you lose that person, do you lose that love forever or do you keep it with you? The film's answer is that you keep the love with you. The last shot of the film is the wife moving down a path not sure where she is heading, happy to just be moving forward. Never did I realize I would live that character's journey and the film would be a prelude to where I am.

## December 7

As I print out a newly created credit card account listing, a piece of paper gets caught in the printer and I pull it out with difficulty. I notice the plastic tape on the lid holding the ink cartridge is twisted, I tear and remove it - big mistake. My printer is no longer printing. I get up to make a phone call and my phone is not allowing me to make a call. I pause, feeling a bit overwhelmed at the moment and think, "This is a cinematic moment." It is certainly symbolic of where I am emotionally and psychologically. I am feeling emotionally tired, a bit spent, and vulnerable to the slightest little challenge. I can't linger in this discouragement as it is a big weapon and I won't be defeated. I realize I am tired in this moment. Time to talk with God. I want him to know I don't blame him for Carol's death or any of this, I'm not mad at him. I just need some help here, an intervention. I'm not even looking for a sign, I just need some help in this moment, in this exact time in my life. I feel good speaking to Him. I will also need to continue speaking with myself.

# December 14

As previously mentioned, I have a newfound awareness of how little things can be emotionally triggering. After we moved to New Jersey, whenever we would go shopping at Livoti's, a popular food store in this area, Carol would always buy a container of grated cheese. *Always!* While putting the groceries away during our second, third and fourth visit to Livoti's, I would mention to her that we shouldn't purchase any more grated cheese. Carol would always come back with *"Don't worry about it, I'll use it."* When I clean out the refrigerator, I see several containers of grated cheese with expiration dates that have long passed. There is still one container left with a December expiration date. I don't want to part with another item connected to Carol. I think about how crazy it is that containers of grated cheese can have that much meaning.

I am aware there is a larger, psychological thing going on. If I keep the expired grated cheese in the refrigerator, it serves no purpose other than to provide another emotional trigger of Carol that is hurtful and sad. But if I toss it out, I am letting go of another visual reminder of Carol. I pause and reluctantly toss out all the grated cheese containers and feel a bit embarrassed that I have spent way too much time on such a trivial decision. I'm also aware I cannot go into the same stores and restaurants we went to. When we would go shopping at ShopRite, I would always drop Carol off in front of the store and look for a parking spot while she shopped. Once

I found a spot, I would walk in and look for her down one of the aisles. I cannot imagine myself going to that store alone, walking in and looking, and not seeing Carol in one of the aisles. Now, when I drive by, I purposely look away from these stores as they are a reminder of what is no longer.

I think of a scene from the movie *Cast Away*, where the Tom Hanks character who had been trapped on a desolate island, is finally able to construct a raft strong enough to get him over the large and powerful waves that pummel him and have prevented him from leaving the island. Finally overcoming the force of the waves, he sets sail to nowhere but away from the isolation of the island. On the raft with him is a soccer ball that had been washed ashore when his plane crashed. The soccer ball has his bloodied handprint on it. Driven by his primal need for a human connection, he creates a face out of the blood from his hand and calls the ball *Wilson*. Psychologically, it symbolically serves as his companion, his "human connection". In the scene, Wilson is dislodged from the raft and falls out to sea. Realizing Wilson is no longer on the raft with him, he desperately dives into the water and tries to bring Wilson back. The ball continues riding the tide, pulling away from the boat. The distance between them grows larger and larger. There is a moment when he realizes, that the boat that will hopefully take him to a safe horizon, is quickly getting farther away. He must decide to either continue trying to bring back Wilson and risk dying, or go forward toward the boat and continue his journey back to life.

This scene has a newfound meaning to me and where I am at this moment in my life. As the days continue to distance me from the tragic date of Carol's heart attack, as I transition and slowly become accustomed to this new life, I take a moment to pause. I don't know if I want to have that distance. I don't want Carol to be in the *past*. I know she will always be with me in my heart, but we will no longer continue this life journey together.

I understand all too well now that moment of decision for the Tom Hanks character, wanting to stay in the past, but also realizing the need to stay the course, to get back on the raft and move forward and continue towards life. Like Tom, I reluctantly choose to get back on the raft and move toward life.

# December 17

Linda called me today and said she had met with a medium this past Sunday because she wanted to connect with Carol. The medium has a great reputation and Linda was curious to try to communicate with Carol. Linda, Kenny, and their children have been a part of our family for over thirty-five years. Our children grew up together and we have celebrated many holidays and occasions, both joyful and sad together. Linda took Carol's passing very hard. They were like sisters and truly loved each other.

Linda recorded the meeting with the medium and shared the recording with me. There were certainly some intriguing moments and references he mentioned that resonated with me. There were a number of beautiful moments during the hour-long session; one being that the medium said Carol connects with Linda in a very spiritual way like no one else.

I know there are skeptics about this sort of thing and everyone who ever meets a medium is always hoping to connect in some profound way and jump on any *resemblance* of a connection. However, I believe although there are many frauds out there, a select group of people do have a genuine gift, a sensitivity, that transcends the norm and allows them to communicate with a person that has passed.

I thought about that last statement, Carol connecting with Linda in a spiritual way like *no other*. I am glad that moment made Linda happy and brought her some peace. I also paused and thought why didn't Carol say something like that about *me*? Why didn't she say *I* was the one she connected spiritually with the most? I wasn't upset by the message, I truly wasn't; it just made me pause. But the pause also made me question myself. Why am I even thinking this way? Silly, mindless, stuff.

While driving home from Chris's house this evening, I have a brief conversation with Carol. I ask her several questions. *Were you happy, truly happy with me? Are you ok with how I am attempting to deal with this situation? Or not?* It bothers me that I ask these questions. A medium's reading shouldn't cause me to pause and ask these questions. I should know better than that, but I realize how vulnerable I am at this time. I end the questions, and put on Pandora. The first song that plays is our wedding song, *"Endless Love."* I smile and silently thank Carol for her answer.

# December 20

I am becoming more aware that I am not only trying to grasp the loss of my wife, but also trying to understand how Carol's passing has affected my life in its *entirety.* I'm not speaking just about her absence, but how much my world has changed and continues to change. I am growing more aware of the new challenges, both subtle and obvious. How the life choices I make now are moving me toward a different path, a different reality than what I have known.

At work, I have to change my W-2 form from married to single. Just the word *single* is a term I never thought would apply to me again. The last few days I have been exploring areas in Jersey where I could possibly see myself living. My intention at the moment is to put the house on the market in the spring, which means I have to think about moving again, packing, unpacking, learning a new area and doing it as a single individual. After previously not having moved in thirty-eight years, I now might have to do it again in less than eighteen months.

When Carol and I bought this house, we knew it was too big for us, but we didn't buy it just for us. We purchased this house for our children and grandchildren. For our family and friends, to share, to spend our *golden year's* together. That was the purpose and Carol made it a home. Well, that purpose has changed. The house is too big for just me and Danielle has shared with me that she cannot come to the house, not without Carol. A home once filled with life, with the laughter of grandchildren, now silent.

The loss of a mate is not simply about overcoming the pain and sadness of no longer having that person in your life, but also understanding that there will be changes in so many of the things that were normal and consistent in your life. Some plans come to an end, and new plans begin.

## December 21

Danielle scheduled both of us to visit the same medium Linda met with a few weeks back. I wouldn't normally visit a medium. Not that it's against my religion, it's just not my thing. When I need clarity, comfort, or strength, I go straight to the source and speak directly with God. I have always found answers and peace there. So why would I see a medium? I'm going for two reasons; one, I believe this person does have a gift based on his reputation, and two, I guess it's an opportunity to explore a way to connect with Carol. You do crazy things when you hurt and feel vulnerable.

We arrive at the medium's home. He is upbeat and talks about the trials and tribulations he has gone through and how those personal challenges led him to discover his gift. I believe him…or do I *want* to believe him?

Danielle goes in first and I sit in the waiting room. I look out the window and across the street is a small wooded area. All the trees are leafless, barren, and exposed to the cold winter conditions. I find myself staring intently at this image in front of me and realize it's an honest metaphor for me at this moment in my life. I gaze at the trees, branches devoid of leaves, colorless, and vulnerable to the force of a cold and relentless winter's wind.

The branches bend gently, swaying back and forth, but the trees still hold their place. I think once again how cinematic this would be in a scene. It's certainly how I'm feeling. I think about how these trees will once again grow leaves in the spring, regaining their beauty and vitality and becoming stronger as the sun and time restore their full potential. That is my hope for myself as well.

Danielle's session is over and I walk in. The medium is personable and offers me a seat. He once again shares his history for several minutes and I'm wondering, if this is part of the hour I'm paying for? I smile to myself and the thought disappears. It's nice to know I still retain some sense of humor.

He tells me there are a number of souls in the room who want to communicate with me. I share a story with him from my past about Maryann, a girl from my neighborhood who I knew when I was fifteen. I liked her and she liked me; however, we never had an opportunity to get closer or date as, sadly, she was killed in a car accident. I remember feeling a profound sadness for her. I prayed for her every night after she passed and one night, years later, she appeared to me in a dream. In the dream, I am walking with Carol who turns to me and says, *"MaryAnn wants to see you."* Carol leaves and suddenly Maryann approaches. She looks beautiful and has a great light around her. She smiles and embraces me with such a pure sense of love, that when I wake up from the dream, I still feel Maryann's head resting on my chest, the hairs on my arm raised and my entire body tingling. I have *never* felt that sense of pure love. The medium tells me Maryann is the one who connected me to Carol.

He tells me Carol has entered and wants to tell me I am the light of her life and that she already came to me. He asks me if I had a surreal experience at the hospital that let me know she transitioned. I am shocked by this and share the story about my body turning frigid just before Carol passed and believing Carol touched my shoulder at the moment she passed as I was sleeping. He tells me that was her letting me know she transitioned and wanting me to know she would never leave without saying goodbye and that she is finally at peace. I admit I am taken aback by him conveying something so intimate that I would be the only person to know.

The session ends. There are some other specifics he shares that no one would have known, like Carol calling me *The Mayor,* a favorite expression she used because of how often I would meet people. The medium also shares Carol communicated to him that I don't like being alone and that I sit on a bench and speak with her. Both of those statements resonate because one of the additional challenges I am fighting through is indeed being alone for the first time in my life. As I have written, when I stay at Chris and Melissa's home, there is a bench next to a senior citizens home where I sit looking out over a wooded area. It's there for some strange reason that I feel very close to Carol.

When I reflect upon the session, I believe the medium did connect with Carol and some of my other loved ones. There were specific things he communicated that couldn't be a coincidence. He hit on several points and missed on a couple of others.

Overall, what I get from this experience are two lessons; One there is so much we don't know and it's important to be open, and two, when you are grieving, you are vulnerable and embrace *anything* that potentially gives you answers, peace, or an opportunity to connect with the person you lost.

# Winter

## Christmas Eve

This is one of the days I am dreading the most. Christmas Eve was Carol's night. No one did this night better than she did. We would go shopping and start preparing weeks before and Carol would place a huge fish order. She knew just what to order and how much. Christmas Eve usually started in the morning with preparing and cleaning the fish. By the afternoon, there would be a variety of shrimp, lobster, scallops, etc., frying on the stove or cooking in the oven. The smell from the kitchen was a big part of what defined Christmas Eve for us. Carol ran the kitchen like a conductor directing an orchestra. She was in synch with everything. She knew just when to remove what was frying and begin breading something else and I enjoyed watching and assisting her. My job was basically opening up the clams and cleaning crabs. By 5:00 p.m., friends and family would start arriving. Everyone would be looking forward to getting together, enjoying Carol's cooking, and sharing the traditional seven-fish Christmas Eve feast. No one made baked clams like Carol.

As I finish writing that last sentence, a sense of sadness hits me; the reality that I will never taste her cooking again, nor watch her cook with the confidence and love that she put into it for her family and friends is heartbreaking. Writing this journal regularly puts me in a place that reminds me of what was and allows me to visualize those moments and go deeper into remembering and appreciating that time. However, it's a double-edged sword because it also opens a door for profound sadness to enter. Uninvited.

This morning, I awake not knowing exactly what I will do. However, I do know one thing, I need to keep busy and not stay in the house for a long period of time. I take a shower, eat a quick breakfast, and go out to pick up gift-wrapping paper.

A few nights ago, Chris asked if I would be ok with him giving one of Carol's bracelets to his mother-in-law, Lisa. He wanted to give it to her as a Christmas gift from himself and his mother. It immediately resonated that Carol would indeed be happy if he did this. Carol loved Lisa and I just knew she was smiling at Chris's suggestion.

Carol has a good amount of jewelry and I am waiting till more time passes to sit down with Danielle and Chris and address what we should do with her jewelry and clothing moving forward. My thinking is to give the majority of the jewelry and clothing to Danielle and share other pieces with family members and certain close friends she loved. I think it's important to share a part of Carol with those she loved and have no doubt Carol would want this as well.

I take out a few bracelets and lay them on the side of the bed where Carol slept. I ask her to guide me, as I often do now. I select a bracelet to give to Lisa and send a picture of it to Chris and Danielle to get their thoughts. Chris texts me back that the one I selected is the one Lisa gave Carol.

After I pick up gift-wrapping paper, I drive to Chris's and leave the bracelet with Melissa then head home where most of the day I wrap gifts. Initially I wasn't going to buy any gifts this year, but I know Carol wouldn't be happy with that. She would want me to continue the tradition we started when Danielle and Chris were young. Plus, I know she wouldn't want Christmas to pass without me buying gifts for our grandchildren. She was always exceedingly generous.

I finish wrapping the gifts, load the car, and drive to Danielle's house. I'm going to sleep at her house tonight. I don't want to wake up Christmas morning alone at my house, not without Carol. That is just too much. Chris told me he wanted to be alone tonight with Melissa and Anthony. As much as I want us to be all-together tonight, I honor his request and we plan on being together Christmas Day.

The night is uncomfortable and a bit surreal but, strangely, I am not feeling overtly sad. This feeling is confusing to me. Normally at this time our home would be filled with people, eating, laughing, drinking. Am I in denial? Insensitive? Or am I actually starting to adapt to the reality of the situation? Again, more questions I don't have answers to.

Initially, Danielle was going to order food and we would eat together but she calls me as I'm driving to her house and asks me if I'm hungry. She says she will order something for me. I find this surprising but take it that she doesn't want any resemblance of Christmas Eve this year. I understand and tell her I'm not hungry.

When I get to the house, they want to watch *It's A Wonderful Life*, my favorite film. It's been awhile since I've watched it and it's not long before I connect to this film, a film I have watched at least twenty times, in a very different way. I focus on the theme of how one person can positively affect so many people in their life and immediately connect that thought to Carol. She truly did touch so many people's lives. I am blessed to have had her for so many years in my life, sharing a journey, and I recognize that more than ever. I am blessed to have so many wonderful people in my life who love and support me. I stay with the movie's theme that a person can make such a difference in people's lives and embrace it.

My first Christmas Eve without Carol and what do I come away with? Although the pain of Carol not being here is undeniable, so are the wonderful moments we experienced. She made Christmas Eve a special day and those memories, the food, and the happiness of those times will continue to be a part of our tradition and of this evening; it just ended way too soon. Although I can't hold Carol, I can hold onto the memories she gave us. Is this enough? No, but what other choice do I have? Although certainly not the same, it was indeed a *Wonderful Life.*

## Christmas Day

In the early days after Carol's passing, I knew Christmas Day was going to be one of the most difficult days to get through. Sleeping over at Danielle's is definitely the right decision, as I have the opportunity to wake up and see Aiden and Aubrey open their gifts instead of waking up to a silent and dormant house. Witnessing their excitement, pure joy in opening their gifts is heartwarming. As I stated earlier, I have come to realize, no matter the despair I am going through, my grandchildren make my heart smile. Quite amazing.

Later in the day, Chris arrives with Melissa and Anthony along with Larry, Lisa, Andrea, and Frankie. I intentionally pause for a moment to observe these special people. We share our time, happy to be with each other, but once again the undertone of Carol's absence is very much present. I am and continue to be that constant reminder Carol is no longer here with us.

We eat, drink, and share opinions about everything from religion and politics, to the new Star Wars film. I am happy to be with them and happy... just to be happy. Later in the day, we take turns exchanging gifts and Chris gives me a small jewelry box. I can sense everyone waiting for me to open it with anticipation. I open the box and there is a small picture of Carol in a locket. As I shared, pictures of Carol are a trigger especially when they are unexpected. I immediately feel myself reacting emotionally and although I fight hard to stay in control, tears roll down my face giving me away. There is an awkward silence now in the room and with all the resolve I can muster, thank Chris for the locket. He tells me I can either wear the picture or use the chain to carry the crucifix Carol had. In my mind, I think to wear her crucifix. The small picture I will carry in my wallet.

A few more gifts are exchanged and I am back on track. Lisa hands me a small bag. Inside the bag is a framed picture I took of Carol in the hotel hallway when we attended Andrea's wedding in Florida in August. Along with the picture is a poem about the passing of a loved one, how they are still near and they want you to remember the good moments you shared together. This is definitely a one-two combination to the head. Lisa asks me to read the poem, but I simply can't. I can't even talk. I pretend to read it silently but once again tears stream down my face. I catch Danielle and Chris looking at me with sad expressions.

After each of us open our gifts, I walk outside where Chris is. I ask him how's he doing. He tells me there are times when he feels he's doing OK but suddenly something will trigger him and he feels profound sadness. I let him know I am going through the same experience. Grief is a wound that doesn't heal quickly, or perhaps never completely heals without leaving a significant scar. I imagine grief is similar to an addiction. You miss having the person you lost so strongly, emotionally, and psychologically, that the pain of their loss is only temporarily relieved by keeping them constantly close. But this is a challenging moment in the grieving process because the more you linger in this mindset the deeper you fall into depression. Yet, when you attempt to move forward and free yourself from this dark place, it will be confrontational, and sadness will try to pull you back in. Make no mistake, this is a battle between being *engulfed* in the past, and *embracing* the future.

The rest of the day goes along fine. I receive text messages from friends throughout the day and once again embrace the opportunity to be spending time with the people I love rather than being alone. I can't imagine how anyone who loses a loved one can do this alone. Human beings are not meant to be alone and having to deal with grieving the loss of a loved one alone, without being with the people you love, is incomprehensible to me.

I return home, put my gifts away and read the poem. There is a line about *"Life unchanged."* How can that be possible? Life has been forever changed! Poetic words can't cover up this kind of wound. My grandmother once told me, *"God never gives you a cross you can't bear."* I sit home this evening contemplating what she said. At this moment, I feel it's going to take time, love of family and friends, God, and myself to find the strength to continue this journey.

# December 29

Today I start house hunting again. My real estate agent, Rima, scheduled us to view three homes I pre-selected. I have been trying to gain a better sense of New Jersey communities. I see several options to explore. The first is trying to find a "mother-daughter" house where I would live with Chris and Melissa. They also want to move because the taxes on their home are high. My son doesn't want me to live by myself and both he and Melissa lovingly invite me to share a home with them. I am moved by their gesture, but I would never do that. They need their privacy and life together and I need my own private space as well.

A second option is to find my own place. Someplace where I can downsize yet not feel compromised. A third option is to find a community where I don't have to shovel snow, mow the grass, or attempt to fix anything. Rima thinks the second option fits me better and I agree. Lastly, I can also simply stay here.

I have thought long and hard about this decision and will follow a simple philosophy I live by: *As long as I do the work, I have unconditional faith I will be where I need to be.* Nobody wants me to be fulfilled more than God, so why stress about it? When we bought the house in East Quogue, it was only through divine intervention that we found it when we did. Carol had seen another house earlier that was beautiful but I thought it was a bit small and wasn't sure we would be able to rent it. Long story short, because Carol loved that house, I put in an offer and it was accepted. Two days later the owner received a higher offer and asked me to match it or we would have to close within thirty days and I would be in jeopardy of losing my deposit. I turned away from that home and we found the house in East Quogue that was bigger and better, for slightly more money. In so many examples throughout my life this has been the case.

Rima picks me up at my home and sitting in the car, I realize not only is it strange to be house hunting again, but the reality of where I am compared to where I was eighteen months ago becomes even clearer. I think about the times Carol and I looked at homes during the year before deciding on the house in Manalapan. It's so different this time around. Instead of feeling excited, this time it's surreal and empty. Am I really doing this again? Do I *want* to go through all that we just went through?

We visit three homes on the list. One is in an over-fifty-five community which is the home I actually like the best. It's modern, open and would provide me the opportunity to downsize without feeling like I am moving backward. The surprise of the day is as we walk through the community's center, we meet several people playing ping-pong. A group of senior citizens greet me with a robust and friendly familiarity. After a short conversation focusing on what life is like in the community and all the activities available to them, Rima and I give each other a knowing look, understanding that I am not ready to go into a retirement-like environment. This realization makes me pause and acknowledge that although I have been given a new script, I still can write some of the scenes moving forward.

## New Year' Eve

I anticipate this day is also going to be one of the most challenging to get through. I have never been a fan of New Year's Eve. To me, the duality is strange: the past and future coming together at the same time, reflecting upon the year that is ending and feeling hopeful for the year to come. I even wrote a scene in a feature script about a man and a woman in the early stages of a relationship as a New Year is moments away. The man lost his fiancé earlier that year and is alone in a room reflecting about the year, his loss, engulfed in personal sadness in that moment and stuck in the past. The woman enters the room, excited and hopeful about the potential of the year ahead and their future. After a few dramatic and soul-baring moments between the two of them, they find their own personal space together. Once again, it seems I am living the scenes in my films and this year; the yin and yang, the dark and the light, are even more potent, are even more real.

I awake this morning with no expectations of what I will feel this day, nor do I find myself in any strong emotional place. Again, I don't know if this is a good thing or not, just going with the truth of how I'm feeling.

My first stop is to visit my mother at her nursing home in Brooklyn. Lately, every time I see her, she seems to wane more and more, and I never know if it will be the last time I see her. She is happy to see me and the cheesecake I always bring her. She asks how I'm feeling and I tell her I'm feeling sad. She asks me why. I understand she is fading but the question makes me pause. When I tell her it is because Carol isn't here with me, she has no real emotional reaction. She tells me, she didn't realize I loved Carol *that much*. I am surprised by her comment, in fact a bit angry she would say that, but instead of responding, I absorb the comment. Was I not outwardly conveying I loved Carol throughout the years? Is this simply part of my mother's dementia? Do others have the same perspective? Did Carol?

After visiting my mother, I head to the cemetery. The weather is dreary and cold, I guess as it should be reflecting this time. I drive into the cemetery and it is isolated, with no one in sight. I walk to the gravesite carrying a rock from the front yard of our house to place on the headstone.

Standing at the gravesite, reality once again overcomes me. Grief is tricky and cunning, especially when you're vulnerable and in pain. I didn't need to find myself crying to know how much I love and miss Carol but grief lets you know the reality of where you are and not where you *think* you are. It hides in the bushes and pounces like a lion attacking its prey, looking for any opening you give it. I walk this fine line between not wanting to be too aware of providing an opening and ignoring it.

At this moment, I have no specific thought and yet I have a multitude of them at the same time...strange. How can I be here talking with Carol at her gravesite? It is still so surreal. I talk to Carol about a number of things. I tell her how much I miss her, reflect again on her legacy, our children and grandchildren, and how I look forward to having the holidays behind me. I place the rock on the tombstone, which I know is important to her. I wish Carol Happy New Year in heaven and head back to the car. As I walk back, I feel like I am watching myself from afar. I see and absorb every movement but I can't fast forward this scene.

Sitting in the car, I think about the man in my New Year's Eve scene, alone in the sadness of his thoughts, reflecting on the year. In this moment, I am once again a character in my scripts, this time feeling trapped in the past, trying to understand how to get to tomorrow, not sure of the future.

I have dinner at Danielle's, pizza and sandwiches that Chris D picks up from a local restaurant. I talk with Danielle, play with Aiden and Aubrey Lynn, and go to bed at 11:00 p.m. I purposely do not want to stay up and see the new year come in. My final words before falling asleep and putting this year behind me, are to wish Carol once again Happy New Year, pray to God for a happier year ahead, and thank Him for my many blessings. Goodbye to the Holidays and to 2019.

## January 5

Four months since Carol's heart attack. Today I pay off all credit card bills. It's a big weight off my shoulders. Over the last four months, I have written more checks than I have in my entire life.

## January 7

Hard to believe Danielle is celebrating her thirty-sixth birthday. In my bedroom, I have a picture of Danielle and Chris when they were babies and I periodically look at that picture and pause to think about how they have grown into such wonderful people. During this time, they have been incredibly loving and supportive.

I come home from work, go to Carvel and pickup a birthday cake, two birthday candles in the shape of the numbers three and six, and head to Danielle's house. We light the candles several times because Aiden and Aubrey each want to blow out the candles separately and then sit down to eat the ice-cream cake. I try to get a sense of how Danielle is feeling since this is her first birthday without her mother. I am pleasantly surprised to see she is doing OK, smiling with the kids and talking comfortably. I go home that night feeling happy that she seems to be finally healing, admiring her strength and overall feeling very proud of having such a daughter. Later that night, as I'm about to go to sleep, I receive a text from Danielle. She tells me she wanted to take the time to talk but couldn't and just wanted to say she feels blessed to have me as a father, loves me, and will always have my back. Tonight I go to sleep with tears in my eyes - only this time, for the first time in a very long time, for a happy reason.

## January 9

I have dinner with a friend and colleague, Stacy, who is teaching in our department this fall. We had spoken briefly about her class and I wanted to know how it was going and she also had some questions about the spring semester, so we decide to meet after work. I am late meeting her and Stacy is gracious and friendly. Within a short amount of time, we are in a free-flowing conversation. I learn that her husband passed away seven years ago. I tell her about Carol.

We spend the next three hours talking about the journey and process of grief. So much of what Stacey experienced, I can relate to. I come away with a better understanding that my own process is not unlike what others have experienced and I have a better sense of what to expect down the road. Our conversation brings more clarity about this journey and what is yet ahead. Is this impromptu meeting a coincidence, divine intervention, or simply life happening?

## January 12

I have always been keenly aware of, and curious about, the circumstances around events in my life and trying to determine if there was ever a possibility of a different outcome. On the day my brother was killed in a motorcycle accident, it was raining. He asked me if he could take my car to work out. I told him I had a dentist appointment, and he could take the car when I came back. Being impulsive, he took his motorcycle. All these years later, I still see him on his red bike, riding past the house, and me, looking through the second-floor window shouting at him not to go. I think of him

65

because I have thought about what I could have done to prevent both his death and Carol's.

In Carol's case, she had been on heart medicine ever since she'd had pneumonia seven years earlier. Throughout those seven years, I would often ask her to speak with her primary doctor to re-evaluate her medicine and dosage. Carol was so fearful of doctors she experienced *"white coat syndrome,"* a condition in which a person's blood pressure spikes when they are in a doctor's office. During the years, Danielle, Chris, and I would often ask her to visit the doctor but she always adamantly refused.

There is a distinct connection between my brother and Carol in terms of how I think about their choices and the circumstances of those choices, and that is *free will*. It's a topic I have discussed, debated, and argued with others about. We're not victims of fate, and I don't believe our lives are pre-determined. It's our free will that allows us to make life choices, and the choices we make have their own individual path and destiny. Carol and Frank made choices, simply, not to listen to logic and reason. I'm not angry with either of them for their choices. Both did not want to die. Frank was stubborn, Carol fearful.

Soon after Carol's passing (a phrase still so difficult, so surreal, to say or write), I contact her primary doctor and ask him why she wasn't seeing a cardiologist. He explains the issue with Carol was more about her nerves than her heart. I struggle to understand the logic and reason behind the doctor's response. I also struggle with myself. How much stronger should I have been in forcing her to go to the doctor, especially during that last month? Why didn't I realize she wasn't experiencing panic attacks but really the issue was her heart?

My friend and colleague, Mike, told me his wife, who researches family genealogy, researched Carol's family tree and discovered that Carol's mother, Katie, passed away at sixty-two and her grandmother on her mother's side passed at sixty-eight, the same age as Carol! The news of this stuns me. Why didn't I know this? Was Carol aware of this? If she was, why wouldn't she share this with me or be more proactive in taking care of herself?

These questions are in front of me and I try my best to be honest with myself. The bottom line is that if I had *any* inkling of Carol's family history, had any sense she might be having heart issues, I would have carried her on my shoulders to the doctors. If I knew my brother was going to ride his motorcycle in the rain, I would have cancelled the dentist appointment. But it's not about looking back and trying to make sense of things, or asking whose fault it was, it's about understanding that they made their choices freely, based on their own personal motivations, and sadly, there were tragic consequences to those choices.

In the aftermath, I find I also have a choice regarding how I view the decisions my brother and Carol made. I can be angry with them and myself, I can blame them for not listening, and myself for not being more proactive. Or I can accept their choices knowing neither anticipated the deadly consequences, and give that acceptance to myself as well. Whether motivated by stubbornness or fear, they were both innocent victims of their decisions because they never factored in the dire consequences. I can choose to accept that the same is true for me.

## January 15

Four months into this journey, I find myself in a reflective mind-set. I remember snippets, visual vignettes of Carol and our history together, and a montage of life moments that make me both happy and sad at the *same* time. Some of these images come from pictures in the house or on my cell phone; others are etched in my mind. Images of happy life moments: Carol and I together in Saint Thomas, family holidays, or simply moments I captured from my cellphone of Carol holding our grandchildren, which was often. There is also a picture of me, Carol, Danielle, and Chris sitting, smiling, and posing for the camera at some event. The picture sits among others on the armoire in my hallway near the front door. Every single day I look at that picture and return the smile Carol gives me in the picture. Once again, it is a moment of feeling happy and sad at the same time, a recurring duality that is new to me and continues to reintroduce itself. But the picture makes me feel connected.

Some of the images in my mind are more painful than others: holding Carol's swollen hand in the hospital, talking to her at the cemetery and on her birthday and our anniversary, and remembering the expressions on Danielle's and Chris's faces as they were saying goodbye to their mother for the last time.

Sometimes I imagine Carol sitting in the same chair on the kitchen island when I'm eating alone and seeing nothing but an empty chair. This also happens periodically when I'm driving and look over to see an empty passenger seat. There are times I sit on the couch and see her playing the Letter Soup game on her phone and then the image is gone. I not only reflect on these images from our history but I also think about the things we didn't get a chance to do, like going to Italy, taking a cruise, attending future birthdays, communions, marriages of our grandchildren, watching our children grow older, and growing old together.

I try to stay in the present as much as possible. As I have often shared in this journal, I cling tightly to my family, faith, and friends who share a part of themselves with me just about every day. I stay with the memories for a short time, but I can't linger in this place for too long. It's damaging, *debilitating*. There is a delicate and dangerous balance here that I'm learning to manage as I walk this tightrope without a net.

One of the important aspects of writing this journal is to end each entry with a sense of discovery. What have I learned about myself going through a certain experience or moment during this time? Was there something of relevance that I discovered? Was there an epiphany that gave me clarity? A lesson learned? Although there have certainly been lessons and discoveries that presented themselves, sometimes the fact is, there are no lessons to learn. There are simply times when one has to go through the process of grief, without any discoveries. You get your butt kicked, endure the painful moments, pick yourself up, catch your breath, and just feel grateful you come out of these times ready for a new day, perhaps in some strange way, stronger and more battle-tested.

# January 18

I go to Barnes & Nobles looking for a new book to read and find myself buying a cookbook. One of my objectives this year is to learn how to cook. With the exception of eating over at my daughter's or son's house, I have been eating takeout, or pre-cooked meals, and I don't want to continue doing that. If I can learn one new appetizer, entrée, or dessert recipe a week, that would be a good thing.

I'm sleeping over at Daniele's tonight because we were invited to Linda and Kenny's house for dinner Sunday and thought it would be good if we all went together. My grandson Anthony is under the weather, so Chris and Melissa aren't able to come.

Carol had some money in her 401K account from working part time, and I know she would want me to split what she had with Chris and Danielle, which I did. Danielle used a portion of the money to buy furniture for her guest bedroom that serves as my room when I sleep over. Danielle says this was her mom's final gift to her and she wants to show me what she bought. She takes me upstairs, along with Aiden, and I am immediately impressed with her furniture choices. Not surprised because she learned well from her mom.

Looking at the nightstands, I notice there are pictures on each. I immediately focus on a picture of Carol and me at Aiden's first birthday. Carol is sitting down and I am standing behind her with my hand on her left shoulder. Looking at the picture, I unexpectedly find myself overcome and tears start running down my face. Danielle asks me what I think and when I don't respond, she turns and looks at me. She immediately understands and also fights back her own emotions. She asks me if I want her to remove the picture. I take a breath and say no a bit too loud. I notice Aiden looking at me with a sad expression. He turns, looks at the picture, and kisses it. How can I explain this moment? In the same instant, once again there is profound sadness yet profound love. Sadness in yet another painful reminder of Carol's lost presence and knowing Aiden will never share another life moment with her again. Yet there is the purity of Aiden's love for Carol that still resonates and let's me know their love will never end. He will carry her with him all his life.

I don't understand why I was so distraught looking at that picture when I have pictures of Carol throughout our home. The only reasonable explanation I can come up with is I expect to see the pictures in my house; I see them everyday. The picture in the guest room was unexpected and my reaction was similar to the reaction I had when opening the Christmas gifts with Carol's picture. Perhaps a psychologist can articulate why. I can only share the truth of my reaction in that moment.

People who have lost loved ones tell me although time heals the wound, a scar always remains and the pain never truly goes *completely* away. It may lie dormant for long periods of time but you never know what will provoke the pain to suddenly appear. If it's true that love never dies, then neither does the sadness of the loss.

# January 20

One of the ramifications of Carol's passing, and one I started thinking about while spending those two weeks at the hospital, was what to do about babysitting Aiden, Aubrey and Anthony. Carol babysat four days a week. During the last few days at the hospital, we put together a short-term plan. My daughter's mother-in-law, Stephanie, babysit on Wednesdays; Melissa babysits on Thursdays; and I babysit on Fridays. Danielle watches Anthony on Tuesdays.

Today, Danielle tells me Stephanie is going to Florida for the month of February so she will have to put Aubrey in a day care center on Wednesdays. She isn't sure Stephanie can continue baby-sitting, so come the fall, Danielle will be placing Aubrey two days a week in day care. Ramifications of a significant loss are felt in so many ways, to so many people.

# January 22

Danielle calls me this morning crying about missing her mother. I can hear the hurt in her voice and it pains me. She shares that she misses sharing day-to-day conversations, gossip, and discussions about silly reality shows. She recently took the kids to an amusement park and normally she would call Carol throughout the day telling her about what the kids were experiencing. She tells me this in between crying. I know the feeling, when these moments suddenly hit you. They come unexpectedly; they attack you, and then are gone. The reality of this void, the lack of presence, reminds you that you're not there yet, not at a place where you can function normally without thinking about the severity of the loss. Oh, you will have a few moments throughout the day, but the loss is almost always on your mind. You're a walking wound. When does it begin to heal? Does it ever? To what degree?

## January 24

I heard from Nick and Laura, my "train" friends. We plan to try and get together once a month for dinner. I enjoy our time together, along with Nick's wife, Lucille, and Laura's husband, Frank. Nick and Laura are symbolic of this time in my "Jersey" life, as they were the first people I met on the train as I was learning to navigate my way to and from the new house and work.

Nick texts our group for a restaurant recommendation and I suggest a restaurant called 618. Carol and I had gone there for dinner with our new neighbors, Laurie, Ben, Frank, and Gerri, when we first moved to the house and it was good. Everyone agrees and I make the reservations. I don't realize until Laura's mom wants to attend the dinner that I have instinctively made the reservation for six people.

## January 25

This morning I attend mass at a local church, Saint Thomas Moore, and the priest speaks about Christ being the light in our lives and how we as individuals battle between the light and dark in the world and within ourselves. I can't imagine trying to navigate and deal with this type of sadness and loss without Christ in my life. My relationship with Christ has long been my foundation in helping me develop as a human being and has given me a peace and clarity I would never be able to achieve without him. I have had to tap into everything I have worked on throughout my life to get through this horrific time. I don't know where I would be without Christ's presence giving me strength to take the baby steps to even attempt to move forward.

Someone asked me recently if I am angry with God. I am not. I don't blame God for Carol's heart attack or death. If God had to stop all bad things from happening on this planet -disease, tsunamis, death, especially to those who least deserve it -then what's the point of existence, of living, learning, and surviving? I remember when my brother Frank was killed in a motorcycle accident at the age of seventeen, so many people, religious people, blamed God for his death. I understood the question and the anger and hurt behind it; he was so young, his life ahead of him, it was so unfair. The big question was, "Why didn't God prevent it?" Once again, Frank made his choice, and bad things happen to good people; it's part of life. Like Carol, he didn't know his choice was going to cause his death. I know that might sound cold, but it's the reality of our existence, the world we live in.

To me, God is everything good; it's human beings and our decisions that subject the world and at times ourselves to unnecessary horror, destruction, and death. Natural disasters, disease, it's simply part of the playing field called life.

Whenever one speaks about religion, it seems people react strongly either in a positive or negative way. My intent is never to be preachy or proselytize, but to simply share what I have found and how my faith has kept me moving forward. It would be untruthful if I didn't share how important my faith has been. I simply could not do this on my own.

Whatever one's belief system, the important point in one's spiritual journey is to be curious enough to explore, and courageous enough to discover. Everyone can choose his or her own personal relationship to God...or not. Free will is our second greatest gift after life itself. I can *choose* to give into the pain of grief or fight it, move forward, and in some way, become a better individual. Each choice has its own path, its own destiny. For me, without my faith, without God, I would be in a far darker place, in a very different mindset, and a very different person.

# February 1

This morning I drop Chloe off at PetSmart to get groomed. I haven't spoken much about Chloe, who is a Yorkipoo, which is a cross between a Yorkshire Terrier and a Toy Poodle. I remember when Danielle called me while she and Carol were shopping at the Staten Island Mall. They had walked into a pet store and fallen in love with her. We already had a dog, Kaylee, a golden lab, and I couldn't imagine having two dogs in the house and most likely *me* being the one to walk them! After I initially said no, Carol called me and said, "Danielle really loves this dog." Of course, I gave in. My thinking was, "If she loves something this much, why would I deny her?" When Danielle married Chris D, who is allergic to dogs, we wound up keeping Chloe. I smile about this now because over time, Carol didn't get along with Chloe who would often have "accidents" in the house and wake us up during the middle of the night to be walked. Chloe also has a penchant for absolutely never listening!

Chloe has been a great friend during this time. Just having her presence in the house, following me around, or simply watching her sleeping in her bed, or sitting next to me, is more helpful than I can share. Getting up in the morning and seeing her waiting for me, or lying by my feet while I write, is truly a blessing and makes me feel less alone. Chloe was at the house when Carol had the heart attack and I have periodically wondered what she saw during that morning. If only she could talk and share the events of that morning. Silly thought.

After I drop Chloe off at the groomers, I decide to go to Livoti's market, which is in the same mini-mall. One problem with that is it's the same Livoti's Carol and I often shopped in and I haven't been here since she passed. Before going in, I park the car in front of the store and just sit there for a period of time deciding if I really want to go in. I decide not to be dictated to my own fragility and go in. I don't know if I subconsciously avoid the pitfalls, but I am able to buy what I need without too much angst.

Perhaps in some small way this is a sign I am more resilient than I think, although I purposely avoid the fish section because this is where Carol ordered the fish for our last Christmas Eve together.

After shopping, I go to the dentist to get a crown. The bill after my dental plan contribution is six-hundred dollars. Cindy, the receptionist, tells me that when Carol was there, she had a credit of two-hundred dollars so that is applied to my bill and I only owe four hundred now. Once again, Carol is giving even when she isn't even here. It brings a smile and also a moment of sadness.

I arrive home and have a conversation with Rima about what houses I want to scout tomorrow. I'm not seeing much that makes me feel like I'm moving in the right direction. Is it possible that I am meant to stay here?

I finally have a chance to read emails and see an email from Stacy. She shares a list of comments people often make to someone who has lost a spouse: *"I know how you must be feeling," "She is in a better place," "It will get easier as time goes by," "You need to be strong.".* There are over twenty of them and I would guess I have heard at least half of them. I understand people mean well and truly don't know what to say. I realize a new term for me is *widower.* I haven't thought of myself as a widower yet. It's a term I simply haven't grasped yet. Is that unusual? Naive? Simply denial? Once again, so many emotions, too many questions, no specific answers.

# February 5

Five months have passed since Carol's heart attack. As I have noted periodically in this journal, I consistently find it hard to say Carol *passed* or *died.* Saying it out loud seems so surreal, sad, and more painful. I live in a different world now, a very different life, as do Danielle and Chris. We're still trying to figure this out, if we ever fully will, trying to navigate with the intention of moving forward and an eye toward where we will land.

75

September 5th changed our lives, changed everything forever. Just about every day seems like a test of our strength, faith, and ourselves. I want to be open to the discoveries that lie ahead, I truly do. I want to continue to evolve and explore my potential, what I am capable of, and what is in front of me.

If time heals all wounds, there is a side of me that wishes I could just fast forward a few years, yet I know I have to move along this new journey literally day to day, chapter by chapter. This is a natural process that can't be rushed. I am curious as to what is in front of me, where I'm heading and where I will be. I mean, I know myself and bring the truth of myself to everything I do. I trust this will serve me to make the right choices. I have always been aware that I'm a work in progress but this is different, this is a whole new group of challenges, a true test that makes me, in some ways at least, even more curious as to what my potential is. Who I am, and who I am becoming.

This evening Danielle texts me that she found a card Carol sent her when she lost her daughter Aurora during her sixth month of pregnancy. I call her and she reads the card out loud to me and we cry together. Although we are five months down the road, and at a different stage in this grieving process, we are still a raw nerve, never knowing what will present itself that triggers an emotional response. I hear people refer to this time as "*the grieving period*," yet I think this period is so much more. You see, you're not just grieving, you're going through a multitude of psychological and emotional encounters, changes, confrontations, every day. You're trying not only to *understand* what you're feeling, but how you're *reacting* and *why*. Somewhere in this mix, buried beneath each initial encounter, is what you are learning about yourself and your place in this new world. Sometimes you grasp it immediately; sometimes it takes time to digest.

I was going to end this entry wishing Carol a happy fifth month in Heaven but there's nothing happy about this. I don't even remember the last time I used the word happy. I am still learning how to do this.

# February 11

Today I am celebrating my thirty-fifth year working at the School of Visual Arts. Given that I also graduated from SVA, it will be almost forty years that the school has been a part of my life. I had initially gone to Baruch College but on August 4, 1978, when my brother was killed, I spent a year out of school taking care of my mother and father. In fact, the day we buried my brother, I returned home from the cemetery only to receive a letter in the mail stating that due to my consecutive failing grades in math, I was no longer a matriculated student and was placed on probation.

When I decided not to return to Baruch College and to attend the School of Visual Arts instead, the first time I went to SVA to officially register as an incoming freshman, starting all over again, Carol was with me. I remember the two of us walking into the school and seeing a group of students that were totally different from what I experienced in Baruch, or what we were accustomed to from our Brooklyn neighborhood. It was 1980 and at that time, they would have been called "punk."

After filling out the required paperwork, Carol and I had lunch at a small hole-in-the-wall cafe called *the Birds Nest* that featured food choices that were foreign to us. We laughed and knew this was going to be a different adventure. Thirty-nine years later, Carol isn't here with me to celebrate my thirty-fifth anniversary at SVA, not here to share a dinner, to celebrate the moment we started together, to reminisce and laugh about that day. It's these life moments that are not only meant to be celebrated, but shared with your life partner, the person you love who has been with you from the start, through the good times and the bad. Tonight is another sad reminder I no longer have Carol by my side to share these moments. This evening celebrates an achievement, yet the void of not sharing this evening with Carol by my side, is painful.

What I take from today is not only celebrating my thirty-fifth anniversary at SVA, but also celebrating the memory of sharing it with Carol all those years ago. For both, I am thankful and blessed.

# February 14

Valentine's Day. Yes, it sucks. Glad I'm working from home and babysitting Aubrey Lynn today, who will keep me busy and make me smile. Danielle tells me she cooked a special dinner along with dessert and wants me to stay. I think she doesn't want me to be alone today. She also bought me a Valentine's Day card and wrote some very moving and loving words.

During dinner, Aiden, out of nowhere, says, "*I love Gigi,*" then looks at Danielle and says, "*I know you miss her.*" Where did that come from? Danielle later tells me Aiden was looking sadly at a picture of Carol and me and shook his head. I'm grateful for the moments like these when Aiden lets me know he remembers Carol and can still feel the love they shared. Although I'm sure Carol is happily looking down from heaven knowing Aiden will keep that love with him, I admit that sometimes it's not enough for me. It pains me that the love between them ended too soon and Carol couldn't experience him, and all her grandchildren, growing up, to be part of their birthdays, graduations, weddings. I acknowledge this pain is significant but I don't harbor it too long. I can't. What purpose does it serve?

To many people, Valentine's Day is simply a day created to merchandise, an excuse for companies to make money, and they would be right. To Carol, Valentine's Day had meaning. It was an opportunity to take a moment to pause and recognize your loved ones. Not to take anyone for granted.

I remember early on in our marriage, Carol selected a beautiful Valentine's Day card and, as always, added her own touching words in the card. She would lightheartedly rank my personal notes that often received a good comment. However one particular year, I guess the words I wrote weren't as moving, and she jokingly ranked it a two out of ten. We would laugh about that card every Valentine's Day.

About a month ago, I found a number of holiday cards Carol bought for me, some signed, some not. When I come home from babysitting Aubrey Lynn tonight, I go back to the cards in the drawer knowing that Carol had bought a Valentines Day card for me that she didn't complete. I open the card, which says: *"To My Wonderful Husband on Valentines Day. There are so many different kinds of love, and with you, I have shared them all- the love of friendship, the love of family, and the love of a lifetime. Wishing you a Happy Valentine's Day."* I sense I will read her card every Valentine's Day.

# February 15

Life is a book with each chapter representing a different period along your journey. Each chapter has its own specific time and place along the way. Each scene, a theme that focuses on a particular subtext of where you are in that story. Sometimes you're the writer, totally in control, and sometimes the chapters write themselves, and you're only a background character being driven by the plot, the good and the bad, the yin and the yang, the light and dark. Today feels like a chapter that includes all of the above.

I start the day meeting my friend Cathy for breakfast. She is coming to Manalapan to attend her mother's afternoon luncheon with friends and wants to catch up. I truly value her friendship and feel blessed we have reconnected after so many years. She is a special person to me, and a part of my history. We reminisce about our time growing up in Brooklyn, when life was simpler and lighter, a time in our lives when you don't truly comprehend where you're headed because you're still trying to figure out who you are, let alone life. It's great to see her and remember that time when everyone seemed indestructible and life was simpler and innocent.

After our breakfast, I go to the cemetery and bring a dozen red roses to Carol. I don't want to say I'm bringing them to the gravesite. In my heart, I'm bringing them for her. Carol always loved roses, especially red ones.

It's amazing how quickly standing at the gravesite can bring me back to September 5th. As sad and painful as it is to stand there and speak to Carol, there is a truth in the words that pour out of me that I don't even think about when I'm speaking, a kind of truth that is real and powerful and somehow, strangely sustains me.

After I leave the cemetery, I go back to the old neighborhood, Carroll Gardens, and pass by our old home, 270 Carroll Street, and see major construction going on. It was here that we began our marriage, raised our children, and formed a life together. I see a myriad of images from what seems a lifetime ago, yet strangely, I feel no real emotional attachment and I don't understand why. Why do I feel disconnected from this place now? The place where we spent most of our life together, started our family? Is it a defense mechanism?

In retrospect, I feel this way because I know in my heart it was the right time for us to move. The neighborhood was changing, the house needed work, and Carol and I were looking to move. It was time, the right time, to move on and evolve. I always trust my instincts and I feel good about our decision. The years we spent at 270 Carroll Street were more than good; we created wonderful life memories here. I look at our time there as chapters from the past that feature a different world, a different theme. A place that had its time, but we were ready to move on from. It was time to evolve the story and we were writing new scenes.

## February 16

I am aware that whenever I leave my home to sleep over at my Chris or Danielle's house, I have mixed emotions. There is certainly a sense of feeling blessed and grateful seeing my children, grandchildren, and my son-in-law and daughter-in-law, the continuity of feeling the normalcy of family and sharing in their lives. Yet, there are also moments of sadness about leaving my home, the home Carol created, along with a feeling of being displaced, feeling unsettled, being a nomad.

At this point, I am getting acclimated to staying at the house alone, so I don't have to sleep over my children's homes as often as I used to. Now, I choose to because it provides me an opportunity to spend more time with them and my grandchildren instead of lingering in an empty, quiet house and keeps my promise to Carol to be more involved in their lives.

I find this emotional rollercoaster also happens whenever I leave Chris's or Danielle's house and return home. It's a strange type of uneasiness that comes over me as I drive back home alone, back to an empty house. It's a sort of a nervous, unsettling feeling similar to sitting in a roller coaster and slowly heading toward that first high point, knowing you are going to be coming down fast, nothing too drastic, but there's a sort of a restless anticipation.

I have been through the hardest moments of initially returning to the house without Carol. What can be worse than coming home after burying your wife and sleeping in an empty bed for the first time in thirty-eight years? The harsh reality of returning to such a different and silent home, five months after Carol's heart attack, is still palpable and unsettling, and takes me some time to settle back in by doing a variety of things like; writing checks and paying bills, putting on the radio so the house is not so silent, washing and ironing my clothes, and writing in my office. Once I get through that, I am settled back home, or at least home, as I now know it now.

# February 20

Chris texts me about an experience he and Melissa had tonight. When putting Anthony to bed, they have a ritual where they take turns reading to him in his room until he gets sleepy then put him in his crib to sleep for the night. This evening, while Chris was reading to him, both he and Melissa noticed Anthony looking away from the book, smiling and waving toward another area in his room. He then started throwing kisses in that direction. When Melissa asked him whom he was throwing kisses to, he said *"Gigi."* Chris brought over a picture of Carol and he asked Anthony, *"Who is this?"* and Anthony once again said, *"Gigi."*

People say we hear what we need to hear and believe what we need to believe, but I have no doubt that, Anthony saw Carol and responded to her. We can choose to be closed to the possibilities of things we can't see, hear, or understand and strictly stay within the *realities* of logic and reason as we know it, but I choose to be open to the possibilities beyond my comprehension without being naïve, and embrace all that is possible.

# February 22

Chris, Melissa, and Anthony came to the house today. I bought a new printer and I asked Melissa if she could help set it up for me. It is great to see them all at the house and to actually hear voices resonating throughout the home. I can see Chris and Melissa are initially having a hard time emotionally since it's been a while since they have been at the house. I ask them if they're OK and they are honest enough to share they are having a tough time seeing all of Carol's touches throughout the house but not seeing Carol. I see Chris getting a bit emotional but he is able to overcome his feelings and put up some sports memorabilia for me that I have wanted to display in my office. While Melissa is preparing the printer, a helper icon appears on the screen that is part of the preparation kit. The icon is a woman named Carol.

Anthony is running around, and seeing him in the house, and hearing his voice makes me happy and once again is a reminder how much I miss having those days back when there was so much life here. We have dinner together and I didn't realize until later that this is one of the few times I've actually eaten at the kitchen table. I have been eating on the kitchen island.

Many people have told me a number of times since Carol's passing that grief is a process that doesn't have a right or wrong approach. That everyone has his or her own personal journey. Going through the *reality* of grief, I certainly grasp the truth of that from my own experience, up to this point, and from speaking with others who have also lost their mates. Some recover within a relatively short time, while for others it takes years before they feel they are healthy enough to move forward and explore life once again.

I'm sure there are a number of psychologists who have written their own step-by-step journey of the grieving process, Danielle and my friend Stacy have both shared that there is a recognized five-step grieving procedure, but for some reason, the word *recuperating* resonates with me most. Right now, at this time, I think this word best fits what I'm feeling emotionally and psychologically. Physically, I've gone from weighing 178 pounds to 156 pounds. Similar to someone surviving a major accident, or a substance abuser counting the days they have been clean, I am physically, mentally, and emotionally recuperating from the trauma of Carol's passing. There are times, even days, when I am functioning and feeling like I am healing and then, without any warning, the reality of Carol not being here comes over me like a seizure. It can come in any form, at any time, when I'm walking to work, on the train, passing a restaurant we went to, or seeing her shampoo that is still in the shower. In fact, whenever I pass a diner or the Shop Right store we used to go to, I purposely avert my eyes. I don't know if this is a normal *symptom* of grief, a normal human reflex, or simply, once again, me being in my own head.

Today for the first time, I think about what my own categories of grief have been to this point. Something I wouldn't have been capable of even considering a few months ago.

The first stage for me was *shock*, being hit with an *instantly* life-altering moment I was just not ready to comprehend, yet alone accept. A new reality so emotionally and psychologically shattering, it literally tests every aspect of who you are as a human being. Similar to what I imagine it feels like for someone who experiences war and encounters horrors no human being should ever witness, then suffers all their life with post-traumatic stress disorder.

After the shock of Carol's death, I found myself simply in *survival mode*, just trying to comprehend this new reality that dropped on my head. I was confronted with an overwhelming feeling of loss, sadness, and emptiness as I tried to understand my place in all of this. Just getting through the pain of the day and getting to the next day was an accomplishment. I was simply searching, looking to grasp onto something, someone, that would keep me moving forward. Basically learning how to do this on the fly.

*Guilt* also plays a role in this process, especially when you have *moments* of healing or feeling happy. Guilt will sit down next to you ask, "Why are you smiling, given all that has happened?" I fight through this argument with myself because I value the integrity of my life, and owe it to God, my family and myself to not only move forward but also live. It's not even about keeping busy, but continuing to be curious, and having a desire for a productive life.

I think the next stage I found myself in was *damage control*. Initially identifying the triggers that made me hurt then trying to fight all the things that made me sad: sleeping alone without looking at Carol's side of the bed, avoiding seeing her jewelry, not entering her walk-in closet and seeing her clothes, and definitely not looking at any videos of her. These are all triggers. Understanding that no matter what I do to avoid these things, there are going to be times I have absolutely no control and will simply get beat up. The key is never to *linger* in these moments too long, to acknowledge them when they come, encounter each one head on with a deep breath, but *never* stay with it because it will suck you up like quicksand.

So here is where I currently am, *recuperating*. Recovering from the shock, the emotional and psychological pain, doing the things that put me in a position to start the healing process, and continue moving toward a productive life. Although I don't know what the next stage will bring, I continue walking forward trusting God, my family and myself.

# February 29

I spent a good part of the day getting ready to take sixteen students to Los Angeles as part of an SVA in LA Destinations Program that presents students with an opportunity to meet amazing visual artists in the film and animation industry. This is the first business trip I will take without Carol being here.

Whenever I would go on a business trip, Carol would not be happy. She would always be a bit on the quiet side the day before I was leaving. However, she would still be helping me to prepare, always reminding me of something I was forgetting to bring. When I was running programs in France and Italy, I would ask her to come with me, but she would say; "*Me running around with students isn't a real vacation*," and she was right.

The night before leaving on a trip, we would normally have dinner out. I think about this throughout the day, especially when I'm having dinner alone. The difference in preparing for this trip now is stark, especially given the quiet of the day.

In the nearly six months since September 5th, I guess I have been in Carol's walk-in closet maybe three times. Walking in the room, seeing her shoes, bags, and clothes exactly as she placed them, always makes me feel melancholy and emotional. Today, I have to go into the closet to get the luggage I need for the trip. I decide to bring up Carol's pocketbook, which has been sitting on one of the dining room chairs since that September day. On cue, like a rerun of a scene, I immediately start feeling emotional as I enter her closet. I place her bag in the room and while moving her slippers, I see the familiar small cardboard box that holds our wedding pictures. I haven't looked at these pictures in years and I'm a bit surprised that I haven't thought to look at them during the past six months. After pulling out the first few pictures, I understand why I haven't done it before.

The images of Carol looking beautiful in her wedding dress, the both of us at the church, posing, smiling, is painful yet remarkably joyful at the same time. Again, this strange duality of light and dark competing in the same moment. I still can't comprehend how I can experience such strong and different emotions simultaneously. There we were, frozen in time, happy and hopeful, the start of our lives together. Funny how I have looked at these pictures over the years, yet Carol never seems more beautiful than when I look at them now.

There is truth in the joy of life just as there is truth in the despair I am feeling. Truth has no boundaries, good or bad, no bias or limitations. Life will certainly present the truth of both the good and the bad to you. I just never realized I could experience both of these emotions equally in a moment. Lesson learned.

# March 1

I travel to LA and as I pick up my luggage from baggage claim, I notice the tag on the bag has Carol's name, address, and phone number. I stare at her handwriting and imagine her writing the information on the tag. Yet another unexpected kick in the ribs, but I take this moment to feel Carol is letting me know she is with me on this trip....finally.

## March 3

I sit in my hotel room and find it hard not calling Carol, letting her know how the program is going, or receiving a call from her letting me know how things are at home. It's an empty feeling and I feel isolated. I decide to turn in early.

## March 5

Six months since that September morning. I can't say time has gone by quickly because six months feels about right. But life continues to change quickly. I guess because this date was on my mind, I dreamt about Carol last night. In the dream, we are married. She tells me she has decided to stay overnight in New York for a project, but the reason she is staying in New York doesn't make sense and I'm perplexed by her decision. I call her and she picks up the phone. I ask her why she needs to stay in the city overnight when she can accomplish what she wants at home? When she replies, her voice is faint, and I listen hard to understand what she is saying. For that brief moment, simply hearing her voice is wonderful.

When I wake up, my heart is beating fast. I take a moment to think through the dream and wonder if subconsciously what I'm really asking Carol is, *"Why did you make the decision not to visit the doctor?"* Or is the real question, *"Why did you have to go?"* Maybe it's a combination of both: a decision she made that prevented her from coming back home. The dream makes me question if subconsciously I truly am upset with her because of her decision. Wow – the more I think about the dream, the more amazed I am at the power of the mind to subconsciously reflect the heart.

When I speak with people who have lost someone close to them, one of the things they consistently say is the pain never *fully* goes away. I think what they mean is although you heal and go on with your life, it truly is never the same. How can it be? That's not to say you won't have a good and fulfilling life, it's just not the same.

There is an undeniable wound you carry, and that scar stays with you. It's like swimming in the ocean and getting bit by a shark. You race to get away and you know the shark is following you but as long as you keep swimming toward land, you have a chance. It's when you *stop* that you're in the most danger of not surviving.

When people say, I am *reinventing* myself, my immediate reply is I am not re-inventing myself, I know who I am and I have my foundation. I always feel like I'm a work in progress and have an absolute desire to be engaged in life and to be productive. I am simply doing this in a new script, with a character that is still evolving, learning to be able to live alone, enduring the moments of sadness, recognizing areas of myself that I haven't tapped into, and being open to the experiences and discoveries of the journey that's in front of me. Somehow, I want to come out of this time in my life a better human being.

# March 8

Arrived back in New York last night after our one-week SVA in LA program ended. We have been hearing about a corona-virus that is causing a pandemic and it seems we arrived home just in the nick of time. I have no doubt Carol would have been calling me every day while I was in LA, urging me to head home. Walking out of the airport and jumping in an Uber, not making my usual call to Carol, was certainly on my mind. Coming home to a dark, silent home was…uncomfortable. I immediately put on the lights and TV, but it can't cover up the emptiness of not having Carol greet me as I walk through the door. I go through the mail as I eat the wonton-egg drop soup I picked up on the way home. Another new scene in this new script.

## March 12

For the last few weeks, a comment Carol made before her heart attack has been weighing on my mind. Not sure why now, at this stage of the process, her comment is resonating. Perhaps it was simply waiting on line along with so many other thoughts and questions before reaching me. Or maybe it's just too painful.

When Carol was feeling anxious and nervous during the two weeks before her heart attack, she would say, "*I don't want anything to happen to me, not now.*" My understanding of her words, and what they mean, was primarily about her relationships with her grandchildren and moving into our new home. I think one of the main reasons I write about this today is because Danielle asked me to baby-sit for an hour as she took a business call. While Danielle takes her call, I play with Aiden and Aubrey and after running around for a while, Aiden brings out a stuffed pirate. He looks at the pirate, looks at me, and says, "*You know who bought me this?*" I reply, "*Gigi?*" and he says, "*Yes.*" He looks at me sadly and says, "*I wish she was back.*" At that moment, my heart sinks and I once again fight back tears and immediately think about Carol's words, "*Not now.*" It hurts more than I can share. Carol not being here to enjoy her grandchildren is my biggest trigger.

I tell him how much Gigi loves him and he tells me that he dreams about her. I ask him what he dreams about. He says he sits on Carol's lap and she talks and plays with him, sometimes in a castle. Interesting the timing of this conversation coming at a time when her "*not now*" comment is weighing heavily on my mind. How do I interpret Aiden telling me this now? Is it Carol's way of letting me know she *does* spend time with her grandchildren? That she still has the joy of interacting with Aiden, Aubrey, and Anthony? Knowing Carol, I believe she does spend time with all of them and the comment, "*not now*" only references this worldly existence. She is letting me know she continues enjoying our grandchildren, perhaps even in a more profound way.

## March 14

I notice I am running a bit low on checks from my Capital One account and call to order new ones. At first the woman is simply taking my order and it is fairly routine until I tell her I have to change the names on the checks from both Carol's and my name to simply mine. As I convey this to the woman, I immediately feel a knot in my stomach. She tells me I have to go to my local branch and place the order in person.

I go to the branch and a customer service representative tells me I have to email the death certificate in order to change the names on the account. However, he can still complete the form and get it ready for me. He types for a few seconds and turns the monitor around to confirm what the new check will look like. My name is now *alone* on the check. I stare at the check and the moment is frozen. My name alone on the check just doesn't look right and my emotions tell me it doesn't *feel* right.

It's amazing how the little things you never think about while grieving come up to remind you of your new reality, that what you once took for granted is now a big void. Like opening up a kitchen cabinet and seeing the mixer Carol would use to make the best mashed potatoes I ever had and realizing, I'm never going to taste those mashed potatoes again. Seeing the number of knives, forks, spoons, and dishes that were used all the time, now seldom used. I am still learning where everything is placed in the kitchen: the frying pans, the serving trays, the blender, and all the kitchen accessories.

Just a week before Carol passed, we bought a new dishwasher. I remember when we bought the dishwasher and wish I could go back to that moment in time and change everything. Since then, I think I have used the dishwasher twice. The pantry still has items Carol purchased, canned vegetables, oils, vinegars, coffee, tomato sauce, tea; the freezer still has frozen vegetable packages I haven't touched. I actually hesitate before using any of them. Again, I ask myself a recurring question: Am I crazy thinking this way?

The duality of past and present often collides in unexpected, unpleasant ways. The grandchildren's toys still lay in the toy chest, Yankee candles Carol bought sit in the closet, the shower in our master bathroom still has the shampoo and body cleanser along with her plastic cap placed where she last left them. The bathroom counter holds her items exactly where she last placed them. Moving forward yet not *completely* letting go of the past. Perhaps, it's even clinging onto the past in some bizarre, security blanket way. I have a newfound awareness of the subtle things.

# Spring

## March 20

Covid-19, the disease caused by the coronavirus we all have been hearing about for the last month or so, has arrived big time and become a world-wide pandemic. The virus has grown into something no one could have imagined, or ever thought they would experience in their lifetime. I wonder how Carol would be dealing with this. She would be more concerned about her family than herself.

After arriving back from LA, I go to the office for two days, but the school, like just about every school in the country, soon suspends in-class attendance and transitions to on-line courses. For the sake of logic and reason and trying to suppress the virus from spreading, we are told to work and teach from home.

In addition to schools suspending on-campus classes, non-essential businesses have also been closed and people are being told to stay at home as the pandemic is becoming a monster. Every day the spread of the virus is worse and more threatening. It's been over a week since I started working from home and, like the rest of the planet, trying to *socially distance* (a new term for a new world), to keep family, friends, and myself safe and not give the virus an opportunity to spread.

Yet another moment of transition, where life as you know it changes instantly, abruptly, and you are suddenly thrust into a position where you have to immediately shift even before you know what hit you. I see an analogy between the transition of Carol's passing and the transitioning of this planet as we fight against this virus. I don't often write on Facebook but I share a perspective tonight that I hope might be helpful to others:

*"Starting on September 5th, when I lost my wife, Carol, my life has been in transition and I was challenged to move forward and evolve. The coronavirus pandemic has placed the world and all of us in transition and challenges us to evolve and tap into the best part of who we can be. I understand this challenge now more than ever. I have faith and pray that we can work more closely together, tap into our humanity, and overcome this challenge together."*

As I have stated in this journal, I try with every input, to come away with a sense of clarity or discovery that I have learned from each experience I am having at that moment. Today I was thinking about the year 2020, and perhaps it's not a coincidence that this virus is happening in a year that is the numeric notation for perfect vision. I think the planet is forcing us to take a timeout to look at others in a more human and respectful way. To appreciate and value those in our lives with greater awareness and look differently at what we used to deem important. Perhaps use this time of transition and, instead of finding issues with our differences, embrace them and find a stronger sense of humanity that is in all of us. Like I have found in the months since my own sudden transition in September.

# March 21

Because of the pandemic threatening our planet, people have been told to stay inside their houses and only go out when absolutely necessary to buy groceries, pick up medicine, or walk the dog. Staying inside the house for eleven straight days only to leave periodically gives me more time to feel my solitude, more time to absorb the emptiness of the house, and, of course, to think about Carol. Normally when I'm working, I arrive home around 6:30 p.m., have dinner, read, watch one of the New York sports teams play, speak with family and friends, then head to bed around 10:30 p.m. Weekends, I tend to be out most of the day, so I only have short periods of time being isolated at the house. Being forced to stay inside because of the virus is emotionally and psychologically challenging. Although I realize I am not alone, I admit to feeling lonelier.

Today, Chris D was going to come by the house and bring Aiden and Aubrey Lynn. It would have been the first time Aiden had been at the house since the day before Carol's heart attack. Aubrey has been to the house only once in November when I babysat.

The thought of having Aiden return to the house meant a lot, but because of the current situation, and also having a runny nose, I thought it best to play it safe and not have them come. I continue keeping busy working from home, reading and writing. This is becoming an endurance test.

# March 23

Being self-quarantined at home finally gives me the opportunity to start looking through the plastic containers we stored downstairs when we moved in. The containers are filled with a variety of "stuff" we had to quickly pack when we left our Brooklyn house, including, knickknacks, family photos, Hallmark cards celebrating family and holiday moments, old papers, bills, and the like. I want to start getting rid of all that is old.

Sifting through the plastic containers is like taking a stroll along Memory Lane. I find an album of photos from our family vacation at Disney World in Florida in 1992. Looking at the pictures, I smile not only because of the memory, but how young we all were-and especially looking at my mustache and pulled-up white socks! I see Carol in a variety of poses; by herself, with the kids, and one with just the two of us holding each other. As joyful as it is to remember these special life moments, I can tell you the reality of her not being here in this moment is painful. Seeing her so happy, so joyful, makes me thankful for that time yet I feel immense sadness that we will no longer be creating new memories together. Once again, I experience the duality of happy and sad moments competing with each other simultaneously.

I continue going through the containers and find two Hallmark cards Carol bought for me, both Valentine's Day cards from different times in our marriage. There is a line from one of the cards, "*I love being us,*" that reflects our relationship. As anyone who knows us can attest, Carol and I were so temperamentally different, so emotionally on the opposite sides of the spectrum, yet we loved each other despite our differences. Did we have our disagreements? Of course we did. Argue? Without a doubt. Challenges along the way? You bet. But when all was said and done, we were comfortable knowing we could always express ourselves without trepidation or retribution.

There have been so many moments like today that make me feel both happy and sad at the same time. Moments we shared as a couple, with our children and with our friends. I understand that although I continue this life journey without Carol, I will embrace those memories and take them with me, because they will forever be a part of me wherever this journey takes me.

# April 3

Today, my mother's nurse Andre calls from her nursing home to tell me she has coronavirus-like symptoms, fever and a significant cough. He connects me to my mother via FaceTime and I see her with an oxygen mask on. I take a moment to absorb the sight and talk with her for a short time. Andre takes the phone away and tells me he will keep me updated.

He ends the call and I stand motionless wondering if my wife and my mother will die within seven months of each other? Will I experience that profound sadness once again? My first thought is about the people I need to call. The second thought comes in the form of a question; will I be making arrangements to bury another person I love?

# April 4

Today is my mother's eighty-sixth birthday. After a number of calls, emails, and attempts to connect, I finally am able to Face-Time with her. She actually seems a bit better than yesterday. We have a short conversation and I wish my mother a happy birthday, tell her I love her, and thank her for all she has done. As I speak with her, I wonder: Will this be our last conversation? The last time I wish her a happy birthday? Although she has lived a long life, her health has been compromised for some time and I feel like in some ways, I lost her years ago.

I decide to get out of the house for a while and go to Danielle's to pick up some stuff she is holding for me. Aiden and Aubrey Lynn greet me by yelling "*Pop Pop!*" and once again they brighten my mood. I spend time talking with Danielle about my mother and of course we get around to talking about Carol. I find whenever I speak with Danielle or Chris about Carol, we get emotional. I think it's because we don't speak as much about our feelings, trying to protect and be strong for each other. I think this is a mistake and I will make more of conscious effort moving forward to speak with both of them about what we are feeling but not expressing.

Before I leave Danielle's house, I spend time with Aiden and Aubrey. Aubrey walks over to me, puts her head on my leg, hugs me and unprovoked, tells me she loves me. A beautiful moment, a reminder there are more beautiful moments to come.

## April 5

Seven months since Carol's heart attack. Past the half-year mark and I find that I am keeping score. As the months pass, I feel like I'm running a marathon and getting to the halfway point. I'm tired, emotionally drained, but need to keep moving forward, even if I am literally taking it step by step.

## April 10

This morning Andre calls and tells me my mother's condition has taken a turn for the worse and at this point it is just a matter of time before she will succumb to the virus. He says that if I want to visit her, they will allow me into the hospital, but he emphasizes it's a significant risk since a third of the patients on the floor have coronavirus like symptoms and seven staff members, including him, were sent home with similar symptoms. I want to go but Danielle and Chris strongly tell me I can't take the risk. I ponder going but reluctantly decide not to, honestly, not for fear of catching the virus, but because if anything did happen to me, it wouldn't be fair to Danielle and Chris. I can't put them in that situation.

Andre tells me that he will set up a FaceTime meeting with my mother later in the day. Here is a man fighting the corona-virus, calling me from his home and taking the time to schedule a call for me to say goodbye to my mother. Before we end our conversation, I tell him he is an amazing human being and thank him for his services. I hang up the phone and prepare myself for what will be my final conversation with my mother.

Three hours later, with the help of a wonderful and courageous nurse named Bebe, who used her own iPhone, I FaceTime with my mother and see she is now behind an oxygen tent, struggling to breathe. My mothers face is strained. She is afraid and fighting for breath and her life. My heart breaks that I can't be there to support and comfort her as she has done for me all my life. I call her name and she reacts with a weak voice. I hear what will be her final words to me, *"My son."* This is the last time I will hear her voice, see her, talk with her, the woman who bore me, taught me right from wrong. This is how we will say our final goodbyes? Through a Face-Time call? I tell her how much I love her while tears stream down my face, and I thank her for her unconditional love and everything she did for all of us. I tell her she will soon be with my brother, my father, and Carol. The nurse ends the call and I stand in complete silence for several minutes by the window, alone in my thoughts. Carol's final words to me were *"Goodbye, Sal,"* and now my mother's final words seven months later are *"My son."* Life can be cruel.

# April 11

Today I receive the phone call I have been expecting. At 11:15 a.m., my mother, after eighty-six years on this planet, completed her life's journey and passed on. In less than a year, two of the women I love most in the world, and who unconditionally loved me, are gone. It hurt me not to be at my mother's side; she was always by my side when I needed her. When I was five years old battling a kidney disease called nephrosis, I was admitted to New York Hospital for four months and she traveled by train to the hospital every single day and stayed with me from 10:00 a.m. until 7:00 p.m. when my father would pick her up.

My mother was a colorful character. She made us laugh and would say and do crazy things that made us shake our heads at times. The most important lesson she taught me was how powerful and unconditional love is. She helped shape me as a child, gave me the freedom as a young man to become an individual, yet always let me know there was a loving safe place to go. I believe she is with her parents, my father, brother, her sisters, and Carol. Although I smile when I think about Carol and my mother meeting in Heaven since over the last few years, they were not on the best of terms, but I'm sure they are both now in a loving, forgiving place and finally, getting along.

This is a moment without a true epiphany or discovery. What I have experienced and shared in this journal is life just sometimes kicks you in the groin and forces you to pick yourself up, challenging you and daring you to be stronger. Hopefully, you do come back stronger and, maybe even more important, more appreciative of your life and those around you who helped shape it.

God Bless you Mom, thank you for your love and guidance. Rest in peace.

# April 12

Easter Sunday, a profound day for Christians and for me, as Christ rising from the dead, and defeating death, gives us a chance at salvation and at, once again, being with the people we love who have left this earth before us.

I have lived through many an Easter Sunday. As a young boy my mother would take my brother and me shopping to buy Easter suits and new shoes. We would all go to church and I remember seeing my school friends and their families dressed up. This year Easter is more poignant to me because of the loss of Carol and my mother. Since I can remember, I understood and valued the journey Christ went through for us, and now I recognize and appreciate his journey even more. Because of his resurrection, we also have an opportunity to defeat death. It is this fundamental belief that helps me heal, knowing I will be with my loved ones again. For me, this is not simply a modality, or a belief system to alleviate my pain, but a way of life and a truth that sustains me and I am grateful.

I start the day, with my normal routine: wake up, shave, shower, walk Chloe, have breakfast. But today is a bit different. While walking Chloe, I hear the sounds of geese coming not from the air, but directly from the street. There, walking in the middle of the street, are two geese making whatever sounds geese make. Two people passing by say the same exact thing to me, *"I've never seen anything like this,"* two geese walking on the road, side by side. A visual immediately enters my head of Carol and my mom together, having a good conversation with each other. I smile at the thought and go inside.

# April 15

Today I buried my mother. Because of the pandemic, we can't have a wake or even a church service. We have a quiet burial at Greenwood Cemetery where my mother now lies with my father and brother. Danielle, Chris D, Chris, Melissa, my cousin Frank and his wife, Jenny, share in a short ceremony that seems to go by too quickly. I think about the other times I have been here at this gravesite. My first time was for my grandfather, then for my brother, Frank, when my father was so weak he couldn't even toss a rose on my brother's casket, then again for my uncle Alphonse, affectionately known as Fono, and then nine years ago for my father. Now it's my mother's time. I can't help but think, "When will it be my time? "

I am happy that my mother is now free of pain and no longer feeling lonely. I will remember the good times with her, feeling grateful and blessed for her presence in my life and knowing she is joyful, peaceful and has clarity. Once again, a small consolation to the grief and pain of yet another loss of someone I love.

## April 22

The great British author, C.S. Lewis wrote, *"Sorrow turns out to be not a state but a process. It needs not a map but a history…there is something new to be chronicled every day."* Today, the something new is a stronger sense of feeling alone during this pandemic. Given the forced isolation, I feel Carol's absence even more strongly. I miss sharing this challenging time in our world with her and wonder what her thoughts would have been about the current state of affairs. I wonder what our conversations would be about. I miss hearing her voice, listening to her opinions, sharing mine and getting feedback from her. Being isolated, I miss having her companionship and simply helping each other get through this pandemic. This moment is another reminder, we are not meant to be alone.

## April 25

I had a dream about Carol again last night. This time I see her walking from a distance on a dirt road. I tell her to wait as I go inside to put on sneakers. The next moment, she is sitting on a lounge chair. She looks slim and her hair is curly as if she has come out of the shower and not dried it. I am happy to see her and ask her where she's been? For some reason, I ask her if she was in Atlantic City. She starts to share excitedly where she was but unfortunately, I wake up.

It is great having a sense of being with her again, even for the briefest of moments. Of course, waking up to reality is *not* a great moment. This morning, I start to share my dream with Danielle but she abruptly changes the subject. When I ask her if speaking about Carol bothers her, she says she would rather not have me share the dream. I get it but don't think this is a healthy approach.

I am aware that when I think about Carol silently, I'm OK. I'm even OK speaking with friends about her. However, when I speak out loud about Carol to my family, it's a battle keeping my emotions in control. Not sure why, or if this is a good thing or if this is once again, simply my own process. I think when I speak about Carol out loud, it makes her death somehow feel more real and that brings a different kind of painful reality.

## May 3

Today is Anthony's second birthday. Before I leave to see him, the sun comes out. The temperature is approaching the mid-seventies. I take this opportunity to spend some time gardening in the backyard and getting weeds out of the pots so when I buy flowers, I'm ready to transplant them. This is the time of year Carol and I would go to the nursery and select flowers for the backyard. We always enjoyed doing this, discussing which flowers to buy, where they should go, what colors to get. It was always a welcome sign that spring was approaching.

When I'm done, I bring out one of the patio chairs from the garage and do some reading. Sitting in the backyard, I come to understand that I have gone through three seasons so far without Carol: fall, winter, and now spring. With the exception of the holidays, I anticipate summer will be the most difficult season to get through. Sitting in the backyard without her, not heading out to East Quogue for a weekend getaway, and even a simple thing like not going to her favorite ice cream parlor, Jersey Freeze, are things I am not looking forward to.

Because of the coronavirus, and the fact that Chris is working at Con Ed and can be a risk to me, it has been almost six weeks since I last saw Anthony. Chris and Melissa set up the backyard for a small family party and we keep our social distance but it's tough when your grandchildren want to play with you. When that happens, I put on my facemask and put sanitizer on my hands. Danielle stops by with Chris D, Aiden and Aubrey Lynn. Being around my family, watching my grandchildren play makes my heart smile once again and life, for the briefest of moments, almost feels normal. The exception, of course, is that once again, we are celebrating another family occasion without Carol's presence.

Driving to Chris and Melissa's house, I wonder if there is going to be a moment that Carol lets us know she is there. It doesn't take long. After a few minutes, Melissa comes over to me and shows me a beautiful butterfly sitting on a blade of grass gently fluttering its wings. We smile at each other without needing to say a word. Later, Chris and Melissa pose for pictures with Anthony in front of his birthday cake, and Melissa's sister Andrea shows me a picture she took with her phone. There, an umbrella-shaped rainbow surrounds them perfectly. Isn't the mind interesting? Real or imagined?

I observe Chris and Danielle, thinking how they must be struggling silently, especially Chris at this moment. I play with Aiden, Aubrey, and Anthony and confront another moment of melancholy that Carol isn't here to enjoy them and take part in Anthony's birthday. I quickly get the thought out of my head because I don't want to get emotional in front of everyone, not on Anthony's birthday.

Before heading home, I once again stop by the small park that overlooks a wooded area. I talk to Carol about Anthony's birthday party and this time, speak with my mother as well. I leave the area not so much emotional, but reflective and appreciative for my family and the memories we will continue to make.

I step into my car to head back home and for a brief moment, pause to look over at the empty passenger seat. I visualize Carol sitting there. My stomach literally turns and I get that image quickly out of my head. Whenever I drive to or from a family event or a dinner with friends now, it is uncomfortable, especially driving back home alone and entering the house by myself. Another day, another battle, I wonder if these battles ever end.

# May 5

Today marks eight months since Carol had her heart attack. Eight months since I last saw her smile, asked her advice, or heard her ask me to rub her back. When Carol first passed, and prior to the pandemic, I was out of the house more often. Now, continuing to be confined in the house for longer periods of time, I feel Carol's absence even more. I'm aware of it and try not to stay in these sad moments for too long but it's a challenge not falling victim to the negativity that waits to jump me every chance it gets, if I allow it, especially because I am isolated, hurting, and vulnerable. Realizing this situation is half the battle but the other half is putting up a strong fight.

Nighttime is the most challenging time. I spend almost eighty percent of the day in my office, working from home, reading, and writing this journal. I make dinner and eat on the kitchen island. I simply cannot eat alone at the kitchen table. I always hated eating alone, even when traveling for business. Now it's a part of my daily ritual.

Eight months in, entering our bedroom to sleep is still awkward and unsettling. I am aware of the different energy in the room now, such a significant feeling of loss and isolation. I continue to sleep on my side of the bed, put on the TV, and when I begin falling asleep, shut it off. Every morning, I still make the bed the same way, sheets tucked evenly and comforter neatly placed over the sheet. I place two pillows on the comforter, then two larger throw pillows with matching shams in the middle with a smaller pillow with the letter "*P*" placed in between them.

The struggle may recede over time but nonetheless still continues. As you evolve, so does the battle. When you feel you are perhaps starting the healing process and moving forward, something new like the hint of summer reminds you there is still a long journey ahead of you. I am surviving and becoming battled tested. I am curious to know what I'm capable of in this new life and where I am headed. Today I ask God for the first time: What is to become of me?

I don't want to sound whiney or weak. I realize sharing the truth of what I am experiencing emotionally and psychologically, puts me in a vulnerable place but I am learning that I have to be strong enough to be vulnerable. I see this journal as sort of a responsibility. A responsibility not only for me, but for my family and who ever may read this who is also suffering the loss of a mate or someone they love. I want to connect in a way that let's them know, they are *not* weak but vulnerable… big difference.

# May 6

I receive a text from my next-door neighbor in East Quogue. She asks how everything is going since she hasn't seen us at the house for a long time. I text her back and when I start to write the line about Carol passing, I instinctively pause and struggle to finish the sentence. When speaking about Carol, I choose to use the word "*passed*" instead of the word "*died*." I find saying the word "died" only makes it emotionally harder and perhaps more real in a way. Why do I have that reaction when I am already acutely aware of this reality? Is this my process? Do others grieving have the same experience?

# May 10

Mother's Day, I am very cognizant of all the specific dates on the calendar this year that will challenge me the most. Special dates I should be celebrating with Carol. At this point, I have made it through Carol's birthday, our anniversary, Thanksgiving, Christmas, New Years Eve, Danielle's birthday, Anthony and Aubrey's birthdays, Valentine's Day, and now Mother's Day. I wear these dates as earned badges of emotional and psychological achievements, not to be rewarded, but simply to acknowledge that I am getting through them one at a time. Next will be Chris's birthday on May 13th.

This morning Chris and I go to the cemeteries to visit both Carol and my mother. I drive to Chris' house and see Anthony and Melissa. I hug Anthony and am instantly happy. Being around my grandchildren continues to conquer everything that is dark or sad; it is a primal and instinctive human response. I am also happy of course to see Melissa, who is a wonderful mom, and give her a Mother's Day card.

As we head out, I ask Chris how he's doing, especially given the day. He says, "OK." I admire his strength and heart. We visit Carol first. It's always a punch in the face to go the gravesite. Chris and I each place flowers near the headstone and pray silently together. After a long pause, Chris says, *"Who would have believed last Mother's Day would be the last with mom and we would be standing here?"* This is the first visit where I am not emotionally overwhelmed. Chris digs two holes and plants our flowers. Hopefully they will stay in place and grow.

Before leaving, I thank Carol again for being an amazing mother and loving wife. Danielle and Chris are beautiful examples of her love, generosity, and huge heart. When we sold the house on Carroll Street, she was the one who wanted us to buy each of them their own homes and I agreed. Every time I visit Danielle and Chris, see them in their homes, see my grandchildren playing, I smile silently and know Carol and I gave them a better quality of life. I know she is smiling as well.

Our second visit is to Greenwood Cemetery to visit my mom. I recognize the feelings I have about my mother passing are different in that I actually am happy for her. She is no longer alone, in pain, and depressed. Godspeed, Mom, you are where you always said you wanted to be. I silently thank her for giving me life, being a mentor and setting me on the right course.

Later this afternoon, I visit Danielle. She is struggling and I'm concerned. I know she will fight through this terrible time in her life because she has a strong foundation, but she is still angry and hurting. I ask her how she's doing and she replies, *"Doing as best I can."* She is fighting it. I attempt to talk to her about the day, but she doesn't want to speak about Carol or the day. Fair enough. I walk this tightrope with her. As a family, we have always been quite open and comfortable sharing our thoughts and Danielle has always been opinionated, so when she shuts down speaking about Carol, I know it's not normal, not a good thing. She is stuck, still upset with Carol for not listening to the many times we all asked her to visit the doctor. I once again reiterate the point that Carol didn't know she was going to die and didn't want to die; her fear of doctors was debilitating, and she paid the ultimate price. I tell Danielle she needs to confront this issue once and for all and find a way to resolve it, accept it, to find peace and move forward.

So, as I sit here in my office late at night, reflecting on the day, what do I come away with from the first Mother's Day without Carol? What resonates most is this is going to be a long and challenging journey. Just as the planet is currently in transition from this pandemic, so are we since that

September morning. Life will not go back to being normal and whatever the new normal will be, I hope we come out of this more loving, and embracing everything that is good, no matter which path we take. Not only is grief a process, so is life. How we choose to live, is up to us.

# May 13

Today is Chris's birthday. He turns thirty-three. I have seen him evolve over the years into a wonderful young man, son, and father. He has been remarkably stoic dealing with the loss of his mother. There are times I wish he would open up more about what he is experiencing, but this is who Chris is, and his process. I am blessed to have him as my son. He reminds me very much of Carol, in his demeanor and temperament, but especially with his big heart. I spend a good part of the morning wondering how he is going to feel celebrating his first birthday without his mother.

Early in the day, I am in my home office where, during the fall and winter, I stay the majority of the time especially since the pandemic. I also stay in my office because I don't want to sit on a couch watching TV alone.

I am looking out my office bay window overlooking the backyard, when a humming- bird flies *directly* at eye level in front of my face, stays for a few seconds, then darts off. I absorb the moment and take this as a good omen, as a hummingbird symbolizes eternity, continuity, and infinity. I also reflect what this special moment represents. My first thought is Carol is paying a visit and wants me to know she is always close by and that this pause in our life is just that, a momentary pause. Perhaps it's my mother letting me know love is infinite. Maybe I am just crazy! When all is said and done, it might be none of these things but simply a special moment when a hummingbird stopped by and looked me in the eyes. Once again, it's a matter of choice and I choose to believe what I instinctively feel.

I go to Chris and Melissa's house and her parents stop by along with Andrea and Frankie. I'm always happy to see all of them. Danielle, Chris D, Aiden, and Aubrey join us for a FaceTime "Happy Birthday" to Chris. With the birthday candles lit on the cake, we start singing "Happy Birthday" when suddenly, the front door swings wide open. We all turn to the door at the same time and for a brief moment, stop singing. We finish the song but there's not a person in the room who doesn't believe Carol came to visit and wish her son a happy birthday. I can see Chris fighting back tears. I get a chance to speak with him alone later while we are in the basement. I ask him how he's doing. He tells me it sucks, but for the most part he was doing OK until we cut the cake and the door swung open. That moment was poignant and beautiful, yet sad because once again, it emphasized Carol's absence.

As I head to bed tonight, I reflect on the hummingbird and its symbolism of eternity, the front door of Chris's home opening by itself just as we began singing, and I am appreciative of these special moments. I don't take them as coincidence or for granted, in fact, I *embrace* them as they remind me that not only is love eternal, but so are we. To take such moments lightly, or as coincidence, would be disrespecting the very gift of that moment.

## May 14

During the summer, Carol and I would like to drink a certain rose' every so often. I recently bought a bottle with this in mind and tonight, I opened it. This was the first time I had this particular rose' without Carol. Why am I even *thinking* about this? Again, I'm not sure if this is a normal part of the grieving process, or if I am simply being too aware. More questions without an answer. I fill a glass halfway, lift it up, and toast Carol.

## May 15

Today is the date I was scheduled to travel to France for the SVA at Cannes Film Festival Program, but, because of the pandemic, the festival was forced to cancel its live screenings and transition to online. I have a new and profound respect for *transitions*. They provide an opportunity to *evaluate* and *evolve*. Transitions are never easy, especially when dealing with the grief of losing a loved one. Pain is the starting point during this time of transition, and has forced me to evaluate not only *where* I am in my life, but *who* I am more deeply. Each day is a challenge to overcome the bad, the tragic loss of Carol, yet this time of transition has also presented me with an opportunity to learn how to be a better person, to develop and evolve in ways I never thought of: confronting my fears, living alone, trusting myself, and my faith.

Throughout this journal, and journey, I have written that I am amazed at how the mind works, or at least my mind. Sometimes the briefest of moments can foster such profound emotions or provoke serious thought and reflection. Today I had to sign a rental contract. My realtor sent me the copy of the agreement, noting that she removed Carol's name. The form, which used to have both our names on the same line, now, simply has my name standing alone. I look at my name on the form, as I did with the check, and my heart sinks. It just looks wrong, vacant, yet is very real and sad. These are the little things, the transitions, you never think about that take on so much more meaning when you lose your spouse. Transitions, the good, and the bad have changed me, profoundly and forever.

## May 16

During the week Carol had her heart attack, I found a small packet of sunflower seeds, her favorite flower. I don't remember if they were already at the house, or if I received them in the mail from an organization asking for a donation. What I do remember is promising to plant them in our backyard in the spring. Today I kept my promise and plant them in the backyard. She would have liked that.

Early in the day, I go to a nearby nursery to pick up some plants. This is the time of year Carol and I would visit different nurseries and go back and forth on which plants to buy and where to place them inside the house and in the backyard. Going to the nursery alone is better than I anticipate. It's deciding which plants to buy that is surprisingly awkward. The plants at the house all died and I want to replace them with new plants. Why it took me eight months to do this, I don't know, or maybe I do. I bought the same plants that were originally in the dining room and in the small hallway leading to the backyard and one smaller plant to put near the fireplace. I want to continue the spring tradition, keep things normal, and simply bring some sort of life back in the house. I find replacing these plants a bit symbolic of trying to restore life and beauty back in the house, to revitalize it, and perhaps in some small way, myself.

Buying plants was always the official beginning of summer. This year, it's the start of what I expect will be very different summer. Three seasons have gone by now, each with it's own unique challenges and memories. Summer was the season Carol and I enjoyed the most. Eating out, traveling to the house in East Quogue, spending time with family and friends were the happiest life moments. Of all the seasons, I anticipate summer will be the most challenging. Just thinking about sitting outside in the backyard eating alone, going to the East Quogue home without her, not going for ice-cream at Jersey Freeze, are all things I am not looking forward to. In fact, I am dreading them.

# Summer

## May 17

Normally, on weekends leading up to the Memorial Day Weekend, we would head to East Quogue and start getting the house ready: painting the deck, buying flowers, opening the pool, landscaping, and doing general spring cleaning. We would take the nearly three-hour ride (once we moved to Manalapan) and, in some ways, it was during these long drives that I felt the closest to Carol.

Anyone who knows me can attest I don't enjoy driving long distances. Anything over two hours is too long and I start getting a bit antsy. Carol would always keep me calm whenever she felt I was getting anxious behind the wheel, especially when we were stuck in traffic. There are certain visual landmarks I remember her using to guide me when we initially made the ride to the house. She was my navigator. When I think about that, I realize that it's sort of symbolic for our life together as well. There were so many times we would simply laugh about the stupidest things or spend a good amount of time talking in the car about important matters. I remember during our very first trip to the house, she would make sure to point out which road or highway to get off and where to get on. As we were getting off the Southern State Parkway and searching for highway 27, there were two opportunities to make a right turn. I still see and hear her telling me, *"Not this right, the next one that says Montauk."* I probably would have taken the wrong turn and gotten lost without her. I remember looking at that sign and telling her, *"I will always remember you saying that to me."* On reflection, I am not sure why I said that to her at that moment. A few months ago, heading out to the house with Chris for the first time since September, we passed that same sign and that moment came back to me. My heart sank and that moment brought silence, sadness, and tears. I have lost my navigator.

Whenever we had people renting the house over the weekend, the cleaning company would come to the house on Tuesdays and I would always make sure we went to the house on Wednesdays, after the house was cleaned. Otherwise, I knew it would be a long day if Carol saw how renters sometimes left it. One time we arrived at the house before the cleaning company arrived and all I can say is, it was *not* a pleasant day.

One thing is now clear; in this moment, I can't drive out to the house alone. The drive to the house was our own private time and I am just not ready to do it alone and this bothers me. I need to be stronger because this is causing a dilemma. I need to go out to the house after every renter leaves to inspect for damage and check inventory.

I tell Danielle and Chris that this is going to be the summer where I have to make a decision to keep or sell the summer house. I don't want to sell because the house is an oasis and brings us all together. It was only through divine intervention that we found this house. I have great memories here and want to continue creating new ones, but that is also what makes it challenging. Will the house ever be an oasis again for all of us who loved Carol? Will it ever feel the same way again without her? At this moment, I don't have an answer to that question. I believe wonderful memories are still possible, but it will be different. Perhaps it's best to sell the house and purchase a new home, create new memories. However, the reality is, even if I purchase a new home, we still have to overcome Carol not being with us, not cooking wonderful dishes, not getting tipsy at a winery, not saying goodnight to me as we go to sleep.

Can the old memories you have be separated from the new ones you create or do they just all fit into one big collage of life? I ask myself if I'm being weak about all this. I don't know, I can only express the truth of what I'm currently feeling. Will time make it easier to be back at the house? I don't know the answer to these questions, not now. I *am* sure of one thing: I *do* want to continue coming out here, sharing special times with family and friends, but will they be at this house?

## May 21

I go out to the East Quogue house with Kenny. I have a request from someone who wants to rent the house for Memorial Day weekend. In less than a week, I have the house power-washed, the deck painted, the house cleaned, and the pool opened. I went out to check on the status of the house, clean the barbeque, set up the patio furniture, clean the windowsills, place soap and toilet paper throughout the bathrooms of the house and meet the renters. As I said, something I normally would have done over the course of a couple of weeks.

Being at the house is like reconnecting with a good friend. It has been over two months since I was last here, and that was for only a short time with Chris. I walk through each room and think about all the family and friends who have shared our home. I look at the pictures of past celebrations at the house: pictures of Danielle, Chris, friends, grandchildren, and of course Carol. I find myself once again encountering a duality of emotions, experiencing the happiness and memories at the house, and the void that now lingers ever so prominently.

As I continue to walk through the house, I see Carol in every room, hear her voice, and have flashbacks of things we did. Am I fighting myself here? Should I simply block out these thoughts and stay away from this mindset? How can you *not* experience this sadness and loss?

At this point, I'm not feeling emotionally overwhelmed, I am just fighting not to linger in the sadness that wants to grab me by the throat, while still acknowledging the truth of what I'm experiencing. I know this battle well by now. Again, it's about balance, encountering the sadness, dodging and weaving to avoid getting hit with a knockout punch, and hoping for the bell to end this round.

After spending eight hours at the house, Kenny and I finally head back home. I am grateful and happy Kenny took the time to come out to the house with me. I honestly don't know if I could have done this trip alone. He's a great friend.

As I depart the house, I turn around and visualize Carol standing on the porch watching us leave. Her presence will always be a part of the house and I wonder, moving forward, if we will be able to continue creating life moments here again.

## May 23

Normally, at this time, we would all be out at the summerhouse. In the morning, I would wake up early, get a few yard and estate sales in, pick up bagels and a variety of spreads, and head to the house to make breakfast for everyone. During the day, we would hang out around the pool, go to the beach, fish, or visit a winery. At night, we would all go out to a restaurant and come back to the house and play board games or a game of pool. This summer, none of this will be taking place. I learn that the passing of someone you love changes so many things you never think about. Their death not only affects you and the other people who had been around them, but so many *normal* life activities as well. Grief in a bizarre way is a good teacher, although the lessons learned are always painful.

# May 24

Danielle hosts a small Memorial Day barbeque at her house with Chris, Melissa, Anthony, and me. It's good to see everyone together, all three grandchildren playing and enjoying each other. We sit on the porch, talk, and even laugh. It almost seems normal with the food, conversations, and simply, the family connecting. Not being the one hosting at our house and barbequing feels different, even strange. Not going out shopping, preparing the food, cooking on the grill, is yet another transition.

As we sit around the table, Aubrey spills iced tea and when Chris D bends down to clean it, he finds a feather on the floor. He picks it up and shows it to us. We all know the meaning of feathers. They now have become symbols, a sign that Carol is with us. There have been a number of times where feathers have appeared at what seems exactly at the right moment or special occasion.

One time Aiden took out a box of Jelly Rings, something Carol would always have at the house for our grandchildren, and he said to me, "*Look Pop-Pop, jelly rings just like Gigi in Heaven used to buy me.*" Not even five seconds later, he reached down to the floor and found a feather. He picked it up and showed it to me. We both smiled, knowing the meaning without speaking.

Danielle saves the feathers whenever she finds them. I know she continues to struggle and I follow her inside. I can tell she is not in a good place. She tells me, *She could have been here if she would have listened to us.*" Once again, we have a conversation about this recurring issue that won't go away. I pray she will eventually let this go, move forward, and find peace.

Later in the day, I speak with Chris and Melissa and discuss the possibility of swapping houses with them. My home is too big for just me and the house would be ideal for them and their growing family. Chris is open to making the switch and Melissa sees the logic of making the switch, but both eventually choose not to. I think the decision is the right one since it would be difficult emotionally and psychologically for everyone.

Melissa was the first person I had called to check in on Carol as I ran to catch the train that day in September and I have never had a conversation with her about what exactly she witnessed when she arrived at the house or how she felt. Maybe it was simply too painful for both of us to discuss earlier, and I already knew most of the story from Linda and Kenny. Today, Melissa says something that surprises me: ""*Maybe if I would have arrived at the house earlier...*" She doesn't complete the sentence and I can see she is getting emotional. I tell her it wouldn't have made a difference because as I said, the paramedics were already at the house and she wouldn't have been allowed in. I know how traumatic that day and moment must have been for Melissa. She saw the paramedics take Carol outside to the waiting ambulance. She tells me Carol's eyes were open, which I didn't know.

Memorial Day weekend is coming to an end. I look at each holiday and family event now as getting over another hurdle, another marker on the board. I think to myself, more challenges ahead.


# May 28

Funny how the mind works and how our inner thoughts and fears, come out subconsciously in our dreams. Last night I had a dream about Carol. We are in a house, not ours, and the door leading to the backyard is made of steel. Carol tells me someone is outside with a gun, shooting at the house. I run out and see a few teenagers running away, and start chasing them. As I get near them, somehow they morph into young children. I return to the house and see it's a mess and there is a lot to clean up. Carol is already sweeping and clearing a good portion of the mess. Hmm, what does this dream mean? I ponder this, and perhaps the metaphor is Carol is helping me put the house, my life in order.

Death makes you lose the *physical* component of someone but not their *presence*. Their spirit and the love they gave remains, and is still palpable; it's an essence unto its own. I find I am living the question from my movie Moments: "*When you lose someone who taught you what love is, do you lose that love or do you keep it with you?*" In my film, the answer is that you I keep the love with you. Now I know for sure.

## June 3

I am feeling a stronger sense of loneliness today. One of the things I miss most is the banter with Carol, the opportunity to actually have a conversation or simply get a perspective from her.

In the last month or so, I suddenly have been receiving a number of requests to rent the summerhouse for longer periods of time. I believe a lot of this has to do with the pandemic and people not being able to travel out of the country. I have three young men in their late twenties renting the house this month who have been calling non-stop about a multitude of things. As I patiently address each of them, I think about how Carol would react to their constant requests. I can't help but smile knowing she would not have been as patient.

Since it is a beautiful evening, I think about having dinner in the backyard for the first time since Carol passed, but decided not to because I don't want to sit at the table alone, looking at the empty seat Carol would have been in. I have sat in the backyard reading and had neighbors stop by, but at this point, I can't have dinner alone out there without her. Sitting in the backyard now, I often reflect about those quiet times with her, the simple intimate moments of just Carol and I having dinner, sunbathing, or simply lounging quietly.

I am in the backyard during what is called "magic hour" when the light is golden and diffused. I look at the flowers that only last week bloomed so beautifully, their color purple prominently stating its place and now, so quickly fading away, much too soon. Of course, the immediate analogy is to Carol. I recognize that I am a raw nerve, and I am acutely aware of my vulnerability, which makes me once again pose the question; Is it my vulnerability that is creating so many symbolic moments?

## June 5

It's now been nine months since Carol had her heart attack. Although she officially passed on September 20, it's really September 5th when she left us. No matter how many times I say the word *passed* or mention Carol in the past tense, my emotions rise, and my stomach tightens. Her death continues to be surreal. There are times I just can't completely get my head around this. I often speak to her and get a sense of what she would say. I know she is guiding me, along with my mother. God, I miss her so much. Even writing that line makes me pause, as it is so difficult to even write. Is fighting against how you feel ever a good thing? I know the answer is an emphatic *no*, that it's better to recognize the pain, encounter it and move on, but sometimes, you need to protect yourself from those moments.

## June 6

My son-in-law brings Aiden and Aubrey to the house. It is the first time Aiden has been here since September 4. I honestly didn't know how I was going to feel, happy to have Aiden in the house but sad because Carol is not here to enjoy him. As I write this later in the evening, I felt both emotions. Sad for the obvious reason, but having Aiden and Aubrey at the house was a reminder once again how alive the house used to be, how full of life, how laughter and voices filled the house. It is good to hear and feel that again. Although Carol isn't here, the people who filled the house are here and they are gifts that remind me how blessed I am and how grateful I should be.

I am happy to see them playing with the toys that have been stored in the closet and the wicker toy chest for too long. Aiden immediately goes over to the family room closet and starts taking out toys. He knows exactly where everything is. Watching them both running throughout the house, eating pizza and ice-cream, sitting near the pool, is not only like watching an old favorite movie, but being in it.

I ask Aiden if he remembers Carol babysitting him and he says yes. Aubrey Lynn falls asleep, and I bring her upstairs to the kids' room where Carol would take her for an afternoon nap. I sit on the lounge chair where Carol would often sit and put her to sleep; it makes me feel a sense of continuity, normalcy, and closer to her.

Reflecting upon the day, I know I will *never* lose the memories created in this house, with Carol, Aiden, Aubrey, and Anthony, but I will also never fully lose the pain of their relationship ending much too soon. I am grateful for those memories, grateful Carol experienced the love of her grandchildren, and they experienced her love back. Their love will never die.

# June 12

There are two bathrooms upstairs, the master bath and the guest bath. I primarily use the guest bathroom because it has a larger counter and mirror. Since Carol's passing, I pretty much have left the master bathroom the way she left it. Her two razor blades sit on the hanging rack on the shower head, her plastic head covering and a variety of skin creams along with bath lotions still sit where she last placed them. On the counter, all the items she used- small mirror, cotton swabs, creams-remain in their original places. Isn't this crazy? Another outcome of the psychological mindset of grieving?

For the last nine months, every time I take a shower in that bathroom, my eyes are fixated on Carol's bathroom items and it is always challenging. Emotions range from respecting Carol and leaving them where she placed them, to accepting being sad every time I see them. Today, after weeks of contemplation, I remove her razor blades and shower cap. Taking her razor blades in my hand, knowing she was the last one who touched them, and taking her cap off the shelf, makes my stomach churn, and my heart sink. There is finality in this moment that is hard to put into words, but I have to finally remove them because they are constant visual reminders of Carol no longer being here and it is always so hurtful seeing them. I realize not seeing them will also be sad, but my instincts tell me this is the right decision. These days, I am depending on my instincts more than ever.

When grieving, the materials belonging to the person you have lost: clothes, jewelry, even the rooms they inhabited, take on a strange and different importance that clutter your mind and is heartbreaking. There isn't a playbook for this, no time-table, it's a matter of trusting your instincts and having the courage and faith to eliminate the things that prevent you from healing and stop you in your tracks, at least for the moment.

# June 13

Chris D came over again with Aiden and Aubrey Lynn. This time, they sleep over because Danielle has childhood friends coming by to spend the day with her and sleep at her house. I'm happy because this is something she needs.

It is great to see Aiden once again sleeping in the small bed Carol bought for the kids' room opposite our bedroom, the Mickey Mouse blanket that I washed the day before actually being used, and the crib, also in the room, finally having one of our grandchildren sleeping in it.

## June 14

I wake up at 6:00 am and can't go back to sleep. Suddenly at 6:15, the door opens and there is Aiden, at the doorway with a devious smile, getting ready to do what he ritually does whenever he would sleep over, jump on the bed and wake us up. It feels good to have a sense of normal. Within a few minutes, Aubrey comes in and the two of them are wrestling with me and laughing.

I make breakfast: eggs, bagels, muffins, a little bit of everything. Soon after they finish, they head back home, and the silence returns and lingers heavily. Sometimes there is no more powerful sound than silence, good or bad. I have become accustomed to the silence now in the house, the lack of conversation and laughter. In this moment, I see how far removed I am from what was once normal here and it's yet another harsh reality check.

The rest of the morning I spend reading the newspapers, and watching a virtual mass from Sacred Hearts & Saint Stephen from Carroll Gardens. Afterward, there is a live-stream of Monsignor Massie in an open car, blessing the people of Carroll Gardens. Normally there would be a procession but given the coronavirus, this is the alternative. It is compelling seeing the old neighborhood again, the same streets Carol and I walked with Danielle and Chris in their strollers, looking at the restaurants we patronized. These are the same streets where Carol was born and raised, where we lived for the first thirty-seven years of our lives. A place where we raised our children, where they went to school, made lifelong friends, where Carol and I would go out to dinner, celebrate holidays, family events, and engage with friends. The virtual procession provides an opportunity to travel through a different time in our lives, a sort of Memory Lane trip, and, yes, feel the sense of sadness that always seems to be close by.

Seems the subtext this weekend is how the duality of *past* and *present* moments of your life combine to create a collage of your life. It's the individual images, the short clips that create the scenes in your own life's movie. How you see it completed depends upon how you chose to edit it. Which scenes make it into the final cut? Which ones don't? Makes me wonder, how I will look back at this time in my life years from now, and where I will be as this story continues.

## June 17

Walking Chloe tonight, I do what I often do, reflect. Reflect on where I'm at, how I'm feeling, and where I am heading. It hits me tonight that one specific emotion I have been dealing with since Carol's passing and haven't really written about in depth is loneliness. I know I'm not *alone* in my life, what I'm talking about is just feeling *lonely*. Not having Carol to speak with, be tender with, argue with, laugh and be silent with, is significant. A thought comes to me as Chloe and I walk: Loneliness is the *dance partner* to grief. Grief takes the lead, but loneliness knows every step and dances remarkably well with grief. When grief takes a break, loneliness steps in and takes over.

We're not meant to be alone, not sharing the experiences of a day, the moments, good or bad, with someone. Or not sharing anything but simply being in the same space together. I miss that human connection so much. Missing Carol is separate from this. It's not only missing her and missing doing things with her, it's the actual *void* of the relationship, interaction, sharing thoughts, sounds, touch, exchanging opinions, having conversations; the human connection. Loneliness is its own entity. A vacant, silent, stagnant presence that lets you know it's lingering right there with you, sometimes with every step of this journey.

Nine months into this horrible journey and I'm just writing about loneliness in depth now? I have certainly not only felt it since September, but also fought with it often. Although it's drizzled throughout the pages of this journal, tonight loneliness wants to make sure it is paid its just due. Loneliness is the dance partner to grief. Only there's no music playing and no one to hold onto.

# June 21

I was invited to spend Father's Day weekend with my daughter's in-laws, Jeff and Steff, who recently moved to Center Moriches in Long Island, which is about fifteen minutes from my house in East Quogue. I don't see them often, so it is good to be with them. They are great people who immediately became a part of our family once Danielle married Chris D.

I drive up with Danielle, Chris D, and the kids. They asked me to drive up with them because it makes sense to take one car. As Chris D drives, we pass all the familiar landmarks and I ask myself if I will continue traveling this path alone to my home.

It is great getting out of the house and seeing Jeff and Steff's beautiful new condo. We go to the beach on Saturday, fish on Father's Day and conclude the weekend trip having dinner outside.

When I return home, I read a Father's Day card Carol had given me a few years back that she kept. I knew the card was in the drawer and I wanted reading the card to be the last thing I did before ending this first Father's Day without her.

I read the words on the card, focusing on her handwriting and visualizing her writing the words. I focus on the last sentence, *"Happy Father's Day to My Everything."* My Everything is underlined. She also wrote a short note inside the card. We would always write something extra in cards, and she would always complete her cards by saying, *"Always and Forever."* I would tease her about the word *forever* but now I can attest to it: The love I have for Carol is indeed forever. And today, in this moment, I hold onto that card, and that love, like a life preserver.

# June 22

Sometimes I can simply be sitting, eating, or walking when a thought comes to me out of nowhere, as it did today while sitting in my backyard taking the sun. Grief needs to be respected because the reality of its presence means there is no way you are going to avoid this confrontation. Grief may take a break, but it will let you know in no uncertain terms that it is *not* gone. No matter where you are born, what nationality you are, or what your standing in life, everyone has to deal with grief and those who experience it will attest to its truth, power and its bullying presence.

However, there is a big difference between the *"Presence of Grief"* and the *"Power of Grief"*. Here you get to choose a bit. What I've found is I can't avoid its presence or refuse to acknowledge the painful moments when grief raises its ugly head. And it is indeed ugly, forcing you to confront it head on. It's a necessary step in the healing process to acknowledge the presence of grief. But you also need to move on from it, because if you linger with grief too long, over time it becomes more powerful. The key is knowing when to move on from it and not feed it, learning how to balance between the two. The more you confront grief, the more you learn from each battle and, the stronger *you* get.

# June 28

Nearly ten months since Carol's heart attack, and after much back and forth, I take her winter coat along with two other jackets out of the closet downstairs and place them in her walk-in closet in our bedroom. I wonder if the delay in doing this is once again a sign of my own weakness, or finally having the strength to place her clothes in her own closet. I guess it's a little of both. I move Carol's coat and jackets because every time I open the front closet and see them, the idea of her coats no longer being used, just hanging there, makes me extremely sad.

I walk into her closet and place the coat and jackets on the rack. Every piece of clothing, her shoes and pocketbooks, still remain as she left them September 5. I have been in Carol's closet only a handful of times during these past ten months and each time I go in, it's just absolutely heart-wrenching. It's a morbid museum that pains me and another visual reminder of the void she left behind. Seeing her clothes also reminds me how good she looked wearing them. I can visualize her in almost every article of clothing and shoes and it is painful. I remind myself: *moving forward, not moving on.*

My cousin Frank and his wife, Jenny, call and ask if they can stop by. I love seeing both of them, as they are two beautiful individuals who I have much love for. I grew up with Frank, lived in the same apartment building from when we were seven years old until we were in our early twenties. We have shared a long journey together and many life moments, both wonderful and sad. We have also shared many conversations about faith, politics, and family. When Carol first had her heart attack and I was at the hospital, Frank and Jenny were a steady presence throughout the two weeks, then at my house, and on the phone. Genuine, grass-roots people with a profound spiritual awareness and humanity they live every day of their lives. They talk the talk and walk the walk.

We sit in the backyard, and Frank and I reminisce about the good old days, the pandemic, politics, life in general, and of course Carol. They ask how I'm doing and I repeat a clichéd mantra: *"Taking it day by day."* It depends when I'm asked. I share with them the lonely moments I experience and Frank offers a thought that has resonated with me lately: As human beings, we aren't made to be alone. This is something I have said to people over the years and now it's being said to me. Jenny tells me, *"When you're ready, you will find someone."* Something I haven't given much thought to. My attempt to reply is unexpectedly paused, and I find myself emotionally overwhelmed. I try to reply but I can't. My eyes fill and I'm suddenly feeling sad and awkward thinking about being back on the dating scene. Being with another woman. At this point, although I certainly feel lonely, and miss intimacy, that human interaction, I am not ready to think about trying to connect with someone new. I guess I'm simply trying to find my place in *all* aspects of this new reality, find my way and, in some way, find myself. Another day, another lesson.

## July 4

It's 11:36 a.m. and in half an hour, I will be heading to Chris and Melissa's house, then to Larry and Lisa's new home in Staten Island. From there, we will go to Danielle's house where Chris and Chris D, will shoot off fireworks. The big fireworks, like you see at Disney World!

As I sit here in my office at home, I think about what Carol and I would be doing this morning. We would be setting up the backyard, I would be cleaning the grill and Carol would be getting the food prepped before everyone came over. This new script has different storylines, new plots, but the subtext remarkably stays the same, simply being with the people I love. I would never marginalize or take that for granted. Ever.

We spend most of the day at Larry and Lisa's new home. We eat, drink, and laugh watching Anthony throw water balloons. He is such a character and has a great laugh that makes everyone else laugh. I watch him interact with everyone and see his strong personality come out. Yes, I feel bad Carol is not here watching him and interacting with him. I wonder if she is doing so from afar.

Later at Danielle's house, Chris and Chris D put on an impressive fireworks show. I am glad to see Chris happy, lighting fireworks and enjoying the moment. Through this grieving period, Chris hasn't often spoken about Carol and usually when I attempt a conversation with him about her, it is always brief. Chris internalizes his feelings and I just hope he has found his own healing process. I will continue to check in with him but for now, I simply am happy to see him smiling.

## July 5

Ten months from the day Carol was rushed to the hospital. The double-digit months that have passed feel like a weird sort of an endurance test. Ten months into this grieving process, slowly finding my way in this new script. What parts of the script am I actually writing? Where am I now emotionally and psychologically compared to where I was ten months ago? Although the shock has lessened, the after-effects, the residue of grief, still remains, consistently challenging me on a day-to-day basis. Sometimes in subtle ways, like passing a restaurant we went to and sometimes in more significant ways like lying in my bed at night without my wife cuddling beside me. Throughout these past ten months, as I often write in this journal, I regularly ask myself: Am I creating these challenging moments or am I simply following a process all people who have lost a love one face?

The Kubler-Ross model describes five stages of grief: *denial, anger, bargaining, depression,* and *acceptance.* To be honest, I haven't followed or read too much about the experts analytical or theory-based stages of grief. I don't even know when these five stages are supposed to come along, or for how long they last. Perhaps it's my own ignorance or arrogance, but I don't believe I have followed this model.

I had this conversation a few weeks ago with my friend Stacy who told me about these five stages of grief. The first stage, *denial*, is an initial human reaction to the shock of losing someone you love. This sudden and unexpected reality, this *terrible* heartbreaking pain of loss, just cannot be accepted at first. Yet, how can you deny the reality of what's in front of you? You can't, because the pain shows you how real it is. There were certainly moments when I couldn't believe what was happening, and I still have those moments, but never did I feel I was in a state of denial. Perhaps that in itself might be a sort of denial.

*Anger* is the second stage of grief. I honestly believe I haven't fully experienced this emotion, with the lone exception being the relationship between Carol and our grandchildren ending much too soon. Who am I going to be angry with? God? Carol? As I have stated often throughout this journal, Carol had an immense fear of doctors and it was her free will that made her choose not to go. Have I thought about what I could have done differently? Absolutely. Am I angry with myself for not doing more? The answer, after much self-reflection and contemplation, is no, because I never for a moment thought Carol was having heart issues or that she was in peril during the early part of the morning of September 5. What's the benefit of lingering on these thoughts at this point? It serves no one and only paralyzes you from moving forward. You can't get stuck in the past otherwise you will simply stay there, self-destruct, and never be able to live whatever your new life offers. Anger serves *no one* and only nurtures grief and sadness.

*Bargaining*? I honestly don't understand this one. Am I truly going to say to God, redo what happened and I promise to do something special for you? For the two weeks Carol was in a coma in the hospital I prayed night and day for her to wake up, but I would never insult God or be ignorant enough to bargain with him.

I think of all the five stages, *Depression* is the most obvious and strongest stage and the one most likely to stay with you the longest. As I write this on July 5, I can certainly attest to having moments that make me sad. But it's not a constant, debilitating depression that lingers with me every second of the day. There are a number of moments that make me feel sad: seeing her hair on her brush, looking at pictures of Carol holding our grandchildren, and seeing the sadness in the faces of Danielle and Chris. Those moments makes me hurt.

Regarding the last stage, *Acceptance*, I can't say when I fully accepted Carol not being here, or if I have *fully* accepted it. Even now, ten months into the first year of her passing, I still find it hard to say, "Carol passed" or "died" out loud without feeling absolute sorrow. Her death still feels surreal, or perhaps, too real. Have I accepted it? What other choice do I have? Maybe there is a psychological difference between *intellectually* accepting the death of your loved one and *emotionally* accepting it. I believe it's easier to control the intellectual, logical side more than one's primal emotional reactions. I have to think about that more.

There is another emotion that tried to get into *both* my emotional and intellectual side, an emotion not on the list that, I sparred with: *Guilt*. It introduced itself early in my journey and tried to cling onto me when I was at my most vulnerable. Guilt takes no prisoners, and can play with your head. Did I feel guilty about not being able to save Carol? Yes, but when I looked guilt in the eyes, I knew the truth, and that is, I never thought she was having heart issues. No one did.

This morning Chris texted me to say that he, Melissa, and Anthony are going to stop by. We spend most of the afternoon in the pool and eat lunch inside. What is different about eating lunch inside is actually sitting at the kitchen table. This may sound strange, but I still haven't eaten at the table since September 4. I eat on the kitchen island because I don't want to sit at the table alone and not see Carol sitting across from me. Having a Sunday dinner all together is great and a reminder of something I once took for granted.

# July 6

Today begins the two-week Guest Lecture summer program I started and as I sit in my backyard this morning praying to God, Carol, and my mom to make sure all goes well, a small white butterfly lands on my left shoulder and stays there for several minutes. Just saying.

# July 8

Today is my birthday. I start the day having a quiet breakfast in the backyard, just taking in the beautiful, sunny morning, and being aware of Carol not being here to celebrate this day with me and where I currently am in my life. I reply to a number of birthday texts from friends, family and colleagues, and wonder if I will feel Carol's presence in some way or form today. There is a hummingbird I first saw at my home office window that every once in awhile makes its presence known and I always take it as a good sign that Carol is stopping by to check up on me. I see this humming bird maybe once every two weeks. In the moment I have this thought, I pick up my coffee and see the humming bird briefly stop by one of the potted flowers then dart off. I smile feeling I received my birthday gift from Carol and feeling connected with her for the moment, then instantly feel the separation and sadness.

I spend most of the day babysitting Aiden and Aubrey and answer a number of birthday calls throughout the day. Later, I FaceTime with

Melissa, Chris, and Anthony. I return home and purposely want to end the day reading a birthday card Carol gave me few years ago. I'm glad Carol kept a variety of these cards over the years, representing different holidays, birthdays and other dates that warrant celebrations. I guess she thought of them as keepsakes and I have read them over the last few months on those special dates and they have allowed me to feel close to her. The birthday card she gave me, speaks about gratitude for a life shared and for the love we will always have.

As I sit here at night, getting ready to go to bed, I am grateful for the life we shared, and for her legacy that continues to live on. I close this entry tonight feeling unexpectedly peaceful. Am I emotionally spent, or simply battle tested enough to keep moving forward?

# July 14

Today I pass by a picture of Carol and me dancing at a wedding. The photo is in our family room and I pass it every single day. Today it makes me think about how different my life and world are now. But after a moment reflecting on that thought, I ask myself whether it is truly a *different* life or a *difference* in my life. It may sound trivial, even idiotic, to think about the difference between the words "*different*" and "*difference*," especially in this case but, there is a distinction.

I still live in the reality of the same world I shared with Carol. The home remains the same; work, family, and friends are still in place; so that part of my world, my reality, still exits and hasn't changed. I think there is more of an emphasis on how much of a difference there is in that reality now without Carol. It's up to me to understand this difference and to understand my place in it, what I hold *onto*, and what I move *on* from. It's something I may think about, but the best approach to this is to continue to trust my instincts and ask God for guidance.

133

# July 15

I just finished a book called *Aristotle's Way* by Edith Hall, and toward the end of the book, there is a chapter devoted to how Aristotle viewed mortality. Ms. Hall states in this chapter, *"On Memory and Recollection,"* that the important issue for Aristotle is the difference between *remembering* someone randomly and deliberately *recollecting*. During this period of my life, I clearly understand these differences. There are little, spontaneous moments that will spark a memory of Carol. It could be driving by Jersey Freeze, the ice-cream parlor on Route 9 where we would often go and where I visually remember her sitting in the car eating her favorite ice-cream, a chocolate cone with chocolate sprinkles, or it can be seeing her watch still sitting in its place in our bedroom and remembering how it looked on her wrist. Sometimes when I sit on the couch, I remember her sitting to my left, playing the game, Letter Soup on her cell phone. These memories are spontaneous, painful, and come out of the moment. They are not moments I am purposely recollecting.

Then there are times when I do purposely recollect the life moments we shared. I can't drive to our house in East Quogue by myself because I recollect all those times we shared together in the car, the times when life challenged us and how we overcame those challenges together. Although remembering and recollecting are different, both are painful and *yet,* at the same time, they bring moments to treasure.

# July 21

I am a bit bewildered that my cellphone randomly "pocket dials" people. This morning while walking Chloe, I purposely hold my phone, so I don't accidentally dial someone. A woman in a car slows down and comments on how cute Chloe is. After a minute speaking with the woman, she drives off and suddenly my phone is dialing someone. I look down and the phone has randomly dialed Linda, whom I haven't spoken with in awhile. This has happened a number of times, especially with Linda. So much so that when Linda picks up the phone, the first thing she says now is, *"Did you pocket dial me again?"* We both laugh and agree that it seems Carol wants us to keep in touch.

# July 22

I had another dream about Carol last night. It felt so real, I would call it a visit. We are heading to a concert taking place on a ferry. There is a huge crowd and we are holding hands. She looks great, classy and well dressed as always. I have to go to the bathroom that is downstairs and she is going to walk ahead and get to our seats. I watch her walk a few steps ahead of me and call her name. She stops and I walk over to her and give her a big hug. I tell her I am happy she is there with me. It feels great to hold her in my arms again, to *embrace* her. At that moment, I don't have the mindset that she passed, only that she has been absent for a while and I embrace her and the moment tightly. I immediately wake up and feel the love of holding her, and the pain of waking up without her. I play the dream over and over in my mind.

The dream makes me think about what Carol is feeling. I have no doubt she is in heaven, finally at peace, yet I wonder how she feels about me continuing this journey without her? Is she less peaceful because of the struggles Danielle, Chris, and I are going through? What is she feeling about Aiden, Aubrey, and Anthony? Does she visit them and feel the happiness that was taken away from being here? I believe I know the answer to that last one. I sometimes feel her very close. There are little signs, like the hummingbird facing me directly as I look out my window, a butterfly landing on my shoulder, or a song that I connect to her, *"Charlotte's Song,"* that seems to come on whenever I feel most down. Feathers are another sign, especially for my daughter and son.

If I truly give these questions some thought, I believe Carol feels nothing but love and peace at a level we can't comprehend in this world. I believe she visits and shares her love with us, and is there when we are at our most vulnerable. I guess it simply goes back to faith. Not limiting my personal experience by staying within the parameters of what we can undeniably prove, but believing in something much bigger, a feeling that is genuine and can't be measured with an instrument or determined by data. I can only share how I genuinely feel at these moments, and how strongly they resonate within me. *That* is undeniable.

These questions provoke another question: *What if I was the one who died and Carol was the one left alone, grieving?* She had told me over the course of our life together that if I died, she would never remarry. I believe her because she was very much old-school. I know she would also be heart-broken and battle with grief as anyone would. No doubt, she would devote the rest of her life to Chris, Danielle, and her grandchildren. She would probably spend more time sleeping over their houses but never permanently live with them.

I realize the questions I ask are more about *me* trying to better understand what I am encountering in *front* of me, and *in* me. Trying to grasp this new reality and prepare in the most natural way for what is ahead. My last thought today is the most meaningful, believing Carol is happy and at peace.

## July 25

Today is Aiden's fifth birthday, a big number to celebrate. I have written how much Carol loved him. Aiden brought out a happiness in her that was moving and their relationship to each other was something very special. I think about their relationship even more today, and wonder how I am going to react to Carol not being present at Aiden's birthday party for the first time.

I pick up the catering on my way to Danielle's and arrive at the house around 1:00 p.m. Once again, whenever I go to a family function now, my presence without Carol is palpable and people feel it, *I* feel it. It's never spoken, but it's the old elephant in the room, lingering quietly.

Throughout the party, I'm doing well, not feeling overly down or reflective. When Aiden opens up his presents and then later blows out the candles on his cake, I can't help but take a moment to gaze around the room and wonder if Carol is present, feeling joyful. Surprisingly, I don't feel her close by.

I arrive home at 7:00 p.m., walk Chloe, and go in the backyard to read. I stay in the backyard most of the day during the summer, especially with the weather being so warm and the backyard so peaceful. I embrace the serenity as I would a loved one.

Chris comes over to fix a leaky pipe then Danielle calls me later. I have a sense she is calling because she wants to talk about her mother not being present at her son's birthday. We talk about Aiden's party and the day overall. I want to ask her how she's feeling but hesitate because I don't want to bring her down as she continues to struggle. We talk and Carol comes up in the conversation. She shares that she is still angry with her for not listening to our advice and questions why God didn't spare her. I understand her feelings, pause periodically to compose myself, and continue trying to help her resolve these issues so she can have peace and move on. We finish our conversation and I spend the rest of the night concerned about Danielle and quietly reflecting on our conversation.

Why am I still not able to have a conversation about Carol without getting emotional, yet not be emotional when simply thinking about her? The same questions about the same things! After thinking about this question for a long period of time, I believe I have come to the conclusion that sometimes there are questions that don't *need* to have specific answers. I have to get away from the question, stop seeking an answer, and simply stay with the truth of what I'm feeling. Why do I need an answer if this is what I'm honestly feeling? Who cares if it's me or part of the journey? At the end, it's about the *truth* of the emotion, the experience that resonates inside you. Why allow all the other clutter in? An epiphany?

I end today knowing one thing, how lucky I am to still have such a good life in so many ways that one can easily overlook when grieving. I have loving children who are genuinely good, amazing grandchildren, a great job, wonderful caring family, friends, and co-workers, and, lastly, when all is said and done, myself. A different version of myself certainly, but my life is still a gift worth living.

# July 26

A simple thought came to me tonight while walking Chloe. What is to become of me, Lord? Where am I heading? Am I moving in the right direction? Am I learning the lessons I need to learn that will lead me toward my highest path?

# July 27

People who have lost a loved one, can attempt to share their experience, the trauma, pain, and recovery process, but it's such a personal journey that it can only be shared to a point. There are times when one who is grieving sees and experiences things in a unique, sometimes unconventional way that doesn't seem logical. Simple things can become signs either imagined or true. You feel more vulnerable than ever in your life and although your priorities are reviewed and rearranged to a degree, there is also an honesty to grief that is profound and undeniable. It's like a truth serum. Yet, there is something good about this honesty, this clarity, no matter how painful it can be at times. There is also a simplicity to it; things seem to slow down and, in some weird way, the clarity and honesty that grief brings can also be so clear that it brings a rare form of peace.

Since the weather started getting warmer, I have spent most of my time in my backyard working, reading, writing the journal, and for quiet reflection. The backyard is my sanctuary, a place of serenity that provides me an opportunity to reassess my life at this moment, to better understand my journey, and, most important, myself. I have become familiar with the birds, rabbits, hummingbird, and chipmunks that make their presence known every day and are part of this environment. I jokingly tell my daughter, "If I start giving these animals and birds' names, it's time to put me away!"

In the last week or so, I have seen a new visitor to the backyard, a dragonfly. I first saw it when I was sitting outside at my patio table. I thought it was odd in that it rested on the chair not too far from me and just stayed there. Over the next few days, I saw it when I was in the pool. It would come close to me, touch the water, take off, and return to rest near the pool. It comes just about every day now, sometimes a few times throughout the course of the day. I have become more aware of the dragonfly as it goes to the same patio chair and just stays there for a good length of time! It is black and has a white bottom. Tonight, as I was reading outside, the dragonfly landed about three feet from where I was sitting and once again just stayed there for several minutes. It would periodically flap its wings, fly about three inches from its spot, and land again.

Now, I realize I'm in a sensitive, vulnerable state and my imagination can take me to some interesting places at times, but I have to say, I take this as a symbol Carol is near and watching over me. We used to watch a movie with Kevin Costner called *Dragonfly*. In the story, Kevin Costner's wife is a doctor who dies in a foreign country helping children stay healthy. Costner continues seeing symbolic references to a dragonfly and at the end, we learn that the symbol is meant to send a message to him that the child his wife was carrying when she died, has survived.

Yes, I actually ask myself if this Dragonfly is a symbol that Carol is visiting or am I truly losing it? Is there a message she wants to send me? Maybe I've watched too many movies. I guess it's not about what I *want* to believe, or *need* to believe, but what I *honestly* believe. I believe it's not a coincidence this dragonfly visits me almost everyday. Whatever the purpose or non-purpose, I am grateful for the interaction and it allows me a moment of symbolic connection to Carol.

## July 30

Today I was babysitting Aiden and Aubrey playing with a toy fire engine pretending to rush past the other cars on the table to get to the fire. Creating the sound effects of a fire engine, I loudly say *"toot-toot"* as if one of the firemen on the truck is blasting its horn. A moment after doing this, I remember how I used to tease Carol whenever she would curse. I would make the same "toot-toot" sound meant to signal that she was cursing like a truck driver.

Isn't it *crazy* how, once again, a simple moment like a playful sound effect can instantly trigger me to another time, connecting me to an entirely different emotional place? I guess the wound of grieving someone you love, no matter how far along the journey you may be (or think you are), is just a thin layer away. It's like walking through a field of landmines; sometimes you see the landmine in front of you and can navigate around it, but you never know when that *unexpected* landmine moment will come and set you off emotionally.

# July 31

Since Carol's passing, I have only been to the house in East Quogue a few times and even then, only for a few hours with either my son, or my friend Kenny to check on the house after someone has rented it to make sure the house is ready for the next person renting the house. I have not slept over or stayed at the house since last year.

Since Danielle said she can't come to the house yet, and Chris said he would eventually come but not this summer, I decide I need to spend a few days there as part of my own healing. It pains me that my family is not using this beautiful home, a house that has brought us so many wonderful life moments. The East Quogue house is a friend who is always there and makes you feel good.

My approach is to be with family and friends so I invite my cousin Frank and his wife, Jenny, along with some of my new neighbors who have become friends to spend a weekend together at the house. The trip even includes a fishing trip to Montauk. I scheduled this weekend over a month ago and now the day has arrived.

I honestly don't know what to expect or what the experience will be like staying over, sleeping in yet another bed alone that Carol and I once shared, but I felt it had to be done and I thought this was the way to approach it. I go into the weekend without any preconceived expectations, simply trusting myself and prepared to acknowledge the truth of what I feel emotionally and psychologically.

I also invite Jeff and Steff to the house. I am pleasantly surprised how well everyone genuinely likes each other and connects as if we have all known each other for years. It reminds me of how it used to be at the house, the laughs, playing board games, sitting by the pool, and going out together as a group. It makes me happy and, because of that, makes me feel a bit guilty at the same time. How can I enjoy being at the house without

Carol? How can I laugh playing board games without teasing her? Go to the same restaurants or hang out by the pool with friends without Carol?

There are definitely poignant moments for me during the weekend. I find myself looking at the furniture and remembering when Carol was purchasing it and designing the house. Throughout the weekend, there are times when I reflect and visualize her sitting on the couch, lounging by the pool, or cooking in the kitchen. The biggest question I have throughout that first day is: *How will I feel sleeping in the bed without her for the first time?* The first night is awkward and uncomfortable, but not horrible. I attribute this to being accustomed to sleeping alone in our bed in New Jersey for the last eleven months. It prepared me. Nonetheless, it is still a sad and isolating night.

The next morning for some reason, I open the top drawer on the dresser near Carol's side of the bed. Surprisingly, I find a picture of her mom, Katie, and a separate picture of her father, Charlie, from their wedding day, as well as a birthday card from Carol to me. The card isn't signed but what is written in it moves me. One of the lines reads "...*and before I know it, the time has slipped away.*" I sit on the bed and pause a long time absorbing the words. How poignant those words are now at this time in my life and how they resonate in such a sad and painful way. How can I *not* reflect on how our time together slipped away too soon? So many experiences yet to come, experiences never to be. I can't stay in this mindset; I remind myself it's destructive. I choose to remember the great life moments we shared which now have greater meaning.

# August 5

Eleven months since Carol had her heart attack. Eleven months in a script I am still trying to fully grasp, trying to re-write this story as I go along. I realize that although I have the free will to choose how to move forward, I am like a surfer riding a huge wave, trying to navigate without get sucked under the enormity of this wave towering just over my head. But what am I actually moving toward? Will I continue this journey alone? Am I back to writing this new story or is it too soon to even ask these questions?

One more month before it's been a full year without Carol in our lives. At times it seems like a month ago that she left us, and at times like a lifetime ago… strange. I think in some sad way, getting through eleven months is an accomplishment; however, I'm not sure if it's an accomplishment one should find pride in achieving… or is it?

I am in a different emotional and psychological place than last September. I don't cry as often, I am staying in the present for the most part, and I have settled into a new *routine,* although I still struggle whenever I refer to Carol in the past tense. Eleven months later, and I still struggle just to write it. I believe I am moving forward, healing, but at this point, when people tell me they are proud or impressed with how well I'm dealing with Carol's loss, I honestly don't know how to feel about that. There's a part of me that recognizes the battles I have fought and overcome, and I thank God every day for the strength he gives me, as I would never be where I am without Christ in my life. Yet, the sadness is omnipresent, always lurking, an awkward and uncomfortable absence in my life that is constant and challenges me every day.

When I pause (which is often) and reflect about what has happened and how Carol's passing has affected so many things, the bottom line is I have come to recognize *all* the emotions I am experiencing; the good, the bad, as well as the ugly, are all real and, somehow, all related. Each emotion merits its own personal encounter, and sometimes the encounter is a battle, a fierce battle. When I am conflicted, I go to my base, which simply is being aware of my own truth that cannot be denied or tricked. I rely on this truth as an instinctive guiding force more than ever and embrace it as my own navigational tool that takes me to a safe and honest place. I thank God for without him, I wouldn't have it.

# August 7

When Carol and I decided to sell our home on Carroll Street, we decided we would do so through a 1031 Agreement, which allowed us to use more of the money we received from the sale of the house to reinvest in more properties. Carol made it a point that after the two-year agreement was done, we would gift Danielle and Chris the houses we initially bought for them and I agreed. My initial thinking was to give them each the down payments for their homes and help them along the way, but Carol was adamant and said it was also her grandfather Natale's wish when we inherited the house, that, if we ever sold it, he wanted part of the money from the sale to buy homes for his great grandchildren.

Today, I complete the paperwork that officially gives Danielle and Chris their homes. As I drive to the bank following Danielle and Melissa to have the documents notarized, I speak out loud to Carol "*We did it honey, your wish is done.*" I am able to make her, our, wish come true for our children and for Melissa, Chris D, and our grandchildren. It is a significant moment that is happy and fulfilling in such a profound way, yet sad of course, because Carol isn't here to see this moment happening. No sooner do I finish speaking to Carol, and feeling sad than, a song I have connected to Carol since her passing, "*Charlotte's Song,*" starts playing in the car. This is a surreal moment, a moment of clarity that reminds me of my experience at the hospital the moment Carol moved on. I feel like she is telling me she is indeed present and aware. I can actually feel her happiness and peace and it also gives me a profound sense of peace and fulfillment. It is a personal and intimate connection between us.

## August 17

I had another dream about Carol last night. Once again, we are in a foreign land and with a group of people. I am on the phone ordering food for everyone and asking for everyone's food choices, and when the response is slow, I become annoyed and tell the person on the phone I will call back. When I finish the call, Carol is no longer there. I look for her and find myself on an elevator in a hotel but the elevator isn't working and I can't get to our room.

There seems to be a consistency to my Carol dreams. We are always someplace foreign, either journeying somewhere or already at the place we are traveling to. I see Carol, then lose her and try to find her. You don't need to be a psychologist to figure out the metaphors of these dreams but it is intriguing to me how the subconscious mind works, (at least mine anyway), and let's you know what's truly lying below the surface.

## August 20

I'm glad to have another opportunity for a one-on-one conversation with Danielle. She continues struggling but this time the focus of her anger is at God for not saving her mother. She tells me as a psychologist, she has treated people who have tried to commit suicide several times and were brought back to life so why couldn't a good woman like her mother get that chance? I tell her everyone has his or her own journey and although I understand her question, it is not a question that can be answered, and to blame God and continue to stay in this negative mindset will only prevent her from healing and moving her life forward.

On my way back home, I go over our conversation and a question comes to mind; *What is actually meant by healing?* Are we looking for a permanent place where there is no longer sorrow or emotional pain from the grief we are experiencing and how it is connected to our new everyday life? Or are we only going to achieve that in limited doses moving forward? Are we simply looking to once again be happy without feeling the guilt of being happy? That is a battle of its own; *being happy without feeling guilty about being happy.*

I think the past eleven months have made me battle-tested. I know this journey a bit more now and have become more resilient, as if I've been riding the same rollercoaster over and over again. After all the unexpected twists, turns, and drops, after the hundredth time around, after you have puked and felt dizzy, you adapt and steady yourself. You know where the dips are and brace yourself for those harsh turns, sometimes holding on desperately. At some point, your body, mind, and soul take over and you want to do more than just survive. You want a life, a productive life, not to just make it through another day. You want to be able to share your life and experiences with someone. You just have to remind yourself that you are new to this journey and will continue in this process for a long period of time. You simply can't control the feelings, good or bad; you just prepare for each dip and hard turn that comes your way and hold on tight, sometimes for dear life.

# August 25

As the days draw closer to a year since Carol's heart attack, I pause to see where I am emotionally and psychologically since that day, the fifth of September. I pretty much have established a day-to-day routine that I'm comfortable with, and I re-evaluate where I'm at every so often. I continue to trust my instincts, trust in God, and trust myself with regard to how I am moving forward, healing and making decisions. I want to make sure my motivations are coming from a place of strength and honesty and not from fear or insecurity.

Since that September 5th day, I have learned to do simple things I never did before, like laundry, cooking, cleaning the house, and dealing with the finances. I have written more checks, cleaned more dishes, mopped more floors, and done more laundry this past year than all the years of my life combined. I even bought a stationary bike and an ab-cruncher and try to exercise every day!

I have overcome the hardest challenges: coming back home to an empty house, sleeping in my bed without my wife next to me, and feeling isolated. During these last eleven months I have been introduced to a different side of myself, perhaps in some ways a better side of myself, and with it, a new perspective on what I am capable of achieving and being. I think Carol's death has placed me in a position that forced me to take a deep look into myself, and tap into areas I haven't ever tapped into. Honestly, I didn't even know existed. Areas I needed to explore, simply to survive and move forward. Similar to when my brother died, and I learned the most important lesson of all-never to take anyone or any life experience for granted.

Truth is, I miss the human connection of a life partner, a woman to share my thoughts with, myself with, the way Carol and I knew each other's vulnerability and supported and nurtured each other unconditionally. I miss someone to have a conversation with that reverberates throughout the house, eating together at a table, sharing a joke, simply smiling at each other in a way that says more than words can express, falling asleep holding each other, and of course, intimacy. The challenge is desiring all these things again without the guilt.

I can't deny feeling lonely or the growing sense that, although I'm comfortable *with* myself, I would prefer not to go through life *by* myself. My family, grandchildren, family and friends make my life full, yet there is another side that is void of that human connection shared between two people. I recently started thinking more about this, the balance between the truth of this feeling and also feeling guilty about it. I know what I'm feeling is normal, honest, and healthy, but it's not an easy transition. It's one thing to have a dinner with someone, or enjoy someone's presence, and another thing to actually *be* in a relationship. I also wonder how will Danielle and Chris feel if and when that time ever comes? How will the woman in my life and her family react to me? I have to remind myself once again to do the work and let things happen…or not, in a natural way. Divine intervention once again. Do the work, and know that no one wants you to be more fulfilled than God, so why change that philosophy now?

## August 29

Chris and Melissa finally moved everything out of their home and they, along with Anthony, will be staying with me for the next few weeks until they move into their new home. I am happy and excited for them. They are two amazing people who deserve everything good in life and I am blessed to have them with me for a few weeks.

Melissa's mom, Lisa, was joking with me when she asked if I was going to be OK with the three of them living in my house for the next two weeks after being alone for just about a year. My answer was, "Of course! They can stay here as long as they want," but I understood the question. I have definitely created a daily routine and become accustomed to being alone in the house, or perhaps it is better to say I have *adapted* to being alone, to living by myself.

I guess the real question is: Have I truly started the process of separating myself from my former reality and adapting to what is now my new reality of living alone in a quiet home? Is quiet just a euphemism for "lonely"?

# September 1

I love having the opportunity to spend time with Anthony. It's an opportunity I don't have as much as I would like. In these first few days, we have been playing and laughing and I recognize that there are actual voices resonating in the house. I guess that is one of the things I immediately noticed, in the early stages of being in the house without Carol. Now, the prolonged silence in the house is temporarily gone, replaced by laughter, conversation…life.

I wonder what I will feel when Chris, Melissa, and Anthony leave and move into their new home and I am once again back to being alone in the house. Will I feel the silence even more? Or, as they say, *is this the new normal*? I don't anticipate my emotions, I just trust in what I will feel at that moment.

I go to Danielle's to babysit while she makes a quick run to the dentist. When she returns, I observe her actions and facial expressions, and don't like what I see. There is a restlessness about her, a palpable uneasiness. Danielle is always vibrant, funny, and witty. I need to speak with her and share what I am observing. After a bumpy start to our conversation, we have a good and emotional talk. For the first time I understand she is not only angry, (something I've known for some time), but she has still not yet accepted Carol's passing. Oh, she is fully aware of the reality of the loss, it's just that her heart cannot fully accept it. She shares just how much she misses the daily conversations she and Carol would have about the kids, reality shows, shopping, gossip, and sometimes, nothing at all.

A friend of mine said that since Danielle is a therapist, she should know how to move forward in dealing with her grief. Speaking with my friend Jenn, who is a psychologist, she said that's not the case. She explained that speaking with others about *their* pain is different from experiencing your *own* pain, especially the pain of losing a mother.

I have no doubt, knowing Danielle and her strength and intelligence, that she will move forward toward acceptance and find her way out of this persistent melancholy state. I don't know so much if she hasn't accepted Carol's passing or if she doesn't *want* to accept it. I will continue to be vigilant and pray she finds the peace to move forward.

As the days draw nearer to September 5th, I find myself in a more reflective mindset. I visualize the sequence of moments throughout that day, how everything transpired, and the horrific two weeks that followed. I can see and feel moments of that day vividly, the call from Carol on the train, our last phone call, entering the emergency room, the surreal experience I had at the hospital. Each moment takes me right back to that date and that emotional place.

# September 4

It's hard to believe a year has passed since Carol and I had our last full day together and forty-four years ago since we first met at a communion party. Thirty-nine years as husband and wife. I watch our last full day together like I am watching a movie. Danielle, Aiden, and Aubrey eating dinner with us, Carol and I going to Wegman's, Carol asking me if it's OK to stop at Rita's for ices and seeing her sitting on the passenger side eating her chocolate ice as I wait for mine. These ordinary moments that would normally pass by and be taken for granted, are now permanently etched in my mind.

I can't honestly say if the year has gone by fast. In some ways it seems like it was only a month ago that my world changed in an instant. And yet there are times, after all the stages, all the struggles, when it seems like a different reality. What I can say is never expected that September 4th to be the last full day Carol and I would be together. Who would? No one goes through a day thinking this might be the last time you see a loved one.

My final images of Carol are her sitting on the bed with her back to me, our final dinner with Danielle, Aiden, and Aubrey; the last time we slept in the same bed, held each other, and had a conversation, our last day as husband and wife.

This should be the time when Danielle, Chris, and I are planning Carol's seventieth birthday, a gathering of family and friends celebrating a life shared together. I remember with a smile that I used to tell Carol I married her on her birthday so it would be the gift that kept on giving. I wish I could continue that joke with her, to tell her that really *she* is the one who gave the gift to me.

Today is a busy day as I babysit all three grandchildren with Melissa. It is a full day at the house and spending time with them takes me away from lingering in sadness and reflecting on where we were on this date a year ago. However, I can't let this day go by without taking the time to write and acknowledge what our last full day together means to me. Although I am grateful for the life we shared, it is tragic that this story, our story, ended much too soon.

## September 5

A year ago today, Carol had her heart attack and never woke up to us. Although she officially passed on September 20, she really left us on this date a year ago. One full year through this life-changing time. One full year on a journey I never expected to be on.

I wake up at 6:30 a.m. and think about the start of that day a year ago. I look over toward Carol's side of the bed and I still see her sitting with her back to me, upset about her foot bothering her again. I recall our conversation but nothing else until she called me when I was on the train going to work.

Throughout the day, I look at the clock and think about where I was at various times a year ago. So much of life has changed since then, not only for me, Danielle, and Chris, but for all who loved Carol. My friend Cathy sends me a text message early in the morning to let me know she is thinking about me, as do several other close friends and associates. Their text messages make me feel blessed to have such wonderful people in my life.

Much of the morning is spent painting the family room with Chris. I want to make the room lighter since the color we inherited when we moved in was a bit on the dark side. A few people thought this was a good decision. Another metaphor? A psychological desire to brighten my life, make some changes? I'm not sure and don't want to analyze myself. As always, I am going with my instincts.

I am glad that Chris, Melissa, and Anthony are with me sharing this day together and keeping busy. Chris and I paint without mentioning what today means. I want to get a sense of what he's thinking and normally wouldn't hesitate to speak with him about it, but I decide not to bring it up. We are all aware of the day and feeling the sadness of the day so what would be the point?

In the afternoon, I once again go to the bench near the woods that I have periodically visited near Chris's old house. For some reason, this location continues to make me feel connected with Carol and gives me a sense of peace. I didn't want this day to go by without speaking to her and sharing how I feel about her absence, what we achieved, and where I am currently in my journey a year later. A sad moment but I am resilient and calm as I speak to her. I tell her that I hope she is proud of how I am handling myself, and to continue guiding me.

When I leave, there are tears in my eyes but also a sense of connection and achievement in getting through this moment. Throughout the day, I continue looking at the clock and balancing between seeing the painful images from a year ago and staying in the present.

I think Danielle, Chris, and I will always carry this wound with us and there will be days; and moments that make us feel sad and reflective. But I believe we are now more appreciative, more loving, and not taking anything or anyone for granted. Another lesson Carol taught us that we will always carry with us as well.

As the day winds to an end, I think that I will not consider this an anniversary, since anniversaries are meant to celebrate joyful moments in life. Instead, this day is a somber, reflective, day of missing Carol, as well as a day that marks the accomplishment of getting through one year of pain, sorrow, and daily challenges that still persist. Saying that makes me feel uncomfortable; however, making it to one year without my wife and still being able to embrace all the good in my life, I have to believe is healthy and makes me appreciate more than ever the people and blessings that are a part of my life. I recognize all that is possible. I can't allow grief to engulf my desire to continue to evolve, explore, and discover what is ahead.

# September 7

As opposed to last Labor Day Weekend, I spend most of the morning in the backyard reading then spend time with Chris, Melissa, and Anthony having dinner outside. I barbecue and talk with Chris and Melissa about their plans to move into their new house which will be literally ten minutes away. I want to bring up where we were last Labor Day but don't. Again, what would be the point? Why make Chris and Melissa sad? I'm sure they're having their own personal challenges today.

I review what I wrote about last Labor Day, the last holiday with Carol. The group picture is still so clear and relevant to me. I wish I could go back in time and change history, get off the train, and come back to the house, change this new reality, but it's only for a fleeting moment and I am back to the present ...reality.

So here I am, late at night writing about the day, alone in my office. There is no epiphany to share today, no words of wisdom, or emotional revelation, just another turn of the page as I try to determine where I am in this new script and if I am beginning to understand the theme and beginning to write new scenes in this new story.

# September 11

A year ago today, Carol completed the first week in the intensive care unit in a coma. It was at this point where it was becoming evident that we were not heading in the direction we were hoping and praying for. The reality of what was to come was staring us in the face, *daring* us to keep hoping. I vaguely remembered at that time what this date means for our country as I was totally consumed by what was in front of my family and me. As that first week went by, I watched Danielle, Chris, Melissa, Chris D., Frank, Jenny, Lisa and Larry, Linda and Kenny, lose the glitter in their hopeful eyes, lose hope, and fight the reluctant anticipation of the reality that was coming much too quickly. Losing hope is one of the great tragedies in life.

I remember my conversation with Larry in the waiting room, telling him I didn't have a good feeling about where we were heading, especially after the dreams I had about Carol. I fought to keep hopeful, even though I felt I was in a scene that had already been written and I was simply playing my part, having no control. I would fight against this feeling but would have no choice but to concede the reality in front of me. Today I am in this reality, still reflecting, searching, and praying.

Tonight, Chris, Melissa, and Anthony are spending their last night here before moving into their new home. The weeks they spent here were great but also a reminder of what was lost in this house: voices, presence, laughter, a full life.

Coming home after spending the day with friends and colleagues, I drive on the Long Island Expressway, a route Carol and I often took returning to our Brooklyn home from East Quogue. I remember bits of conversations we had as I approach the Kosciuszko Bridge and how either Carol or I would comment how dirty the underpass leading to the bridge was every time we passed it. I remember making the last turn that would be the homestretch. As I pass the Brooklyn Bridge and the Atlantic Avenue exit where we would get off, it seems like those memories are from another lifetime: well, perhaps not another lifetime, but certainly another life.

## September 12

Last night I had another dream about Carol that also included my mother. Over the past year, I have written about my dreams and how the symbolism of each dream intrigues me. Each dream always seems to include some sort of travel.

The dream last night finds me piloting a small sailboat on a lake where the current is moving very rapidly. As I ride over the waves, I suddenly see Carol windsurfing to my left about ten yards behind me. Concerned she might fall, I navigate the boat toward her, grab her hand, and pull her onto my boat. As soon as I get her on the boat, it suddenly turns into an inflatable raft and starts losing air. Knowing the raft is going to sink, I immediately put Carol back on the sailboard and watch her sail past me while my raft collapses. I get to a group of rocks, hold on, and signal for help from other boats behind me. While I try to draw their attention, I receive a call on my cellphone. It is my mother's voice, barely audible, calling my name.

I think about the symbolism and cinematic visuals of this dream and can clearly see how my subconscious is presenting the subtext of this scene.I am slowly moving along, (in my current life?), when suddenly, I try to bring Carol back into my boat, (my world?), only to have that world collapse and having no recourse, let her go. I cling to the rocks, without panicking but hoping to be rescued. My mother's voice is yet another layer of the loss.

So…what is the symbolism of this dream? A metaphor of my desire to have Carol back? That I wasn't able to save her? Could the raft collapsing be a symbol of feeling my world has collapsed? I'll take the boats coming to help as a positive sign that I will not drown and will continue moving forward. These dreams seem to articulate so well both the emotional and psychological place I'm in. In some bizarre way, these dreams give me a sense of clarity and meaning to the grief I am internally feeling. When I reflect on them, I better understand my place in front of it.

## September 18

I wake up this morning reflective and somber. Tomorrow I will hold a Memorial Mass for Carol with family members and a few close friends attending. Danielle asks me if we really need to do this, to create another moment to feel bad, to go through another wake. I tell her I simply want to recognize that a year has passed since Carol left us. I want to honor her and bring us together not to just remember her, for we will always have her in our hearts, but also to continue to value her memory and presence in our lives.

## September 19

A year ago today I had *that* conversation with Carol's doctor. He told me as compassionately as he could that Carol would not be waking up and coming back to us. Although we had known the inevitable outcome for a few days, actually hearing the words coming out of his mouth, hearing it said out loud, "*She's not going to wake up,*" made the *finality* of that moment devastating and all too real. A year later, I still feel the pain and anguish of that moment.

We had waited two weeks for Carol to open her eyes, to smile or say a word. Day by day, losing hope, yet keeping hope. In that moment, any hope we were clinging to, no matter how small, was defeated. Not only was Carol not coming back, but also the life she and I had lived for thirty-eight years was over; there were no longer pages being written to keep the story alive. The book closed, the script abruptly ending much too soon, much too quickly without the ending we intended.

How do you even begin to grasp this moment from an emotional, psychological, and spiritual standpoint? For me, you can't. Your body, mind, and soul all respond in an instinctive numbing way and you are simply along for the ride with the pain and sorrow it brings. You can't control what your emotions are doing to you at that moment. It's a stunning blow to every sense that makes you - *you*, that makes you human. It just seems so incomprehensible, overwhelming. Although Carol's life ended, not even death can erase the memories, love, and meaning of her life.

This morning we hold the Memorial Mass for Carol. A small group of us comes together to honor Carol but more important, to continue to show our love for her as well. Monsignor Massie, as always, speaks from the heart and reminds us to keep the hope that we will see Carol again and to continue to allow her to live through our thoughts, actions, and in our lives. To remember the lessons she taught us and will continue to teach us.

I speak about what this year of transition has meant to me and how I am continuing to value every moment being around the people I love. I thank Carol for making me a better man, for our two children, and the legacy she leaves. My son, Chris, speaks, and knocks it out of the park. His speech is loving, heartfelt, and moving. His love for his mother and what she taught him is another example of her presence still being alive and viable. Danielle is valiant and shows her strength during the service by speaking and greeting people no matter how she is struggling internally being there. To see so many of the people that were a part of that life, and still are a part of this new one, makes me feel incredibly blessed.

Later that day, a few of us gather at Linda and Kenny's house for brunch and share Carol stories throughout the afternoon that make us both laugh and cry. I am, and will always be, impressed by the number of people she touched, how many people truly loved her, and how much of a role she played in all our lives.

So…what do I make of this day? What do I come away with? I would say that although a person dies, the unconditional love they gave is never extinguished and continues to be the strongest gift they, in this case Carol, gave to all of us. It is real, palpable, and eternal.

When our time on this planet comes to an end, I believe one of the questions God asks us is, *How much did you love*? I know Carol will get an express ticket into heaven with her answer. She has given us the great gift of her love that will stay with us forever or until we are capable of answering that question ourselves.


# September 20

A year ago today at 12:52 a.m., Carol's life journey on this earth ended. This morning I attend a virtual Mass and spend most of the afternoon at Chris and Melissa's new home. Danielle and Chris D stop by and I watch my grandchildren play and run around the house.

I take a moment to observe, or should I say absorb, everyone going about their day; Chris showing my son-in-law his new cinema room in the basement, Melissa showing Danielle the rest of the house, and Aiden, Aubrey, and Anthony running around the house. I take this all in and smile. I can't help but wonder what Carol would be doing if she were here? Probably helping Melissa organize the kitchen or presenting ideas on designing the house. I know Carol is smiling, her heart, her life still evident.

I think the scars we get from grief never fully heal. We continue to evolve and, love and our desire for life does not succumb to this loss, but it will certainly be different, a transitional life redefining itself. For me, I will be even more appreciative than ever for every moment in this new and developing life.

Before heading to bed, I reflect upon the first year without my wife. I feel a sense of achievement that I have not just sustained myself, but emerged tested and stronger. It's like swimming in the ocean for a long time and finally finding a buoy to hold onto for a moment to catch your breath before continuing. I made it this far, and although I have a sense of the direction I'm heading, I don't know what's in front of me, or even lurking below me, but I don't fear the sharks any longer. As long as I continue to do the work, put in the time, make the effort, I trust God will give me the strength, courage, and wisdom to continue moving forward and guide me where I'm heading.

# September 24

I understood when I first decided to write this journal that September 24 2020, one year after Carol's final day on this earth, would be my final entry. A year ago, family and friends stood silently, reverently together at Holy Cross Cemetery as we put Carol to rest. As the final weeks leading to the conclusion of this journal were approaching, I started to think what I would write as the final entry.

Today I receive a letter from Memorial Stone Cutters that the engraving of Carol's name, including her birthdate and date of passing, was completed on the headstone. Included with the letter, is a picture of the completed stone with Carol's name on it. I stare at the image and the *harsh* reality of it all. The image is no longer surreal but unfortunately *too* real. The sadness seeing her name on that stone, especially on the final day of writing this journal, is profound.

So the final *entry* of this journal will be written about a picture of a gravestone with Carol's name on it, and in some stark way, a symbolic final entry, the conclusion of my first year without my wife, Carol, the last period of putting this journal to rest.

## Reflections

A year after Carol's passing, I find that my decision to write this journal is one of the better decisions I have made. Writing about my experiences over the year has allowed me not only to go deeper into the journey of grief, but deeper into myself. Writing about each encounter and understanding my relationship to it, no matter how painful and challenging, has helped me in the healing process and has provided me with a sense of clarity I don't believe I would have achieved if I didn't write this journal.

I didn't want to approach this time in my life in a pedestrian way, to simply accept going through this terrible grieving process after losing my wife. I wanted to better understand my place in all of this confusion, heartbreak, and pain, and better understand myself. I also wanted to document the love and support I personally witnessed and experienced from family, friends, and colleagues both old and new. To explore the personal, emotional, and psychological encounters and real battles that took place during the first year of this process, some of those battles with myself, in a deeper, more profound way than I ever could have imagined. I owed it to Carol, my family, and myself to not simply get *through* this journey, but to give it the respect it deserves; to give Carol the respect she deserves. And to perhaps help others who are also going through the loss of someone they love and the grieving process.

My objective from the start was to write what I was experiencing during the year, not on an everyday basis, but whenever I was confronted with a specific challenging moment that not only introduced itself to me, but tested me in ways I had never experienced. I thought it was important to share these challenging experiences, the truth of them whether good, bad, or horrific, how they presented themselves to me, and my response in front of them. I also wanted to pull back from each journal entry to reflect and share what I learned from a particular encounter. Sometimes, there were moments of true discovery, other times a sense of the surreal. There were also times when I found there was nothing to learn, I was simply getting emotionally and psychologically beat up and finding a way to get to the next day. Hopefully, a bit more battled-tested and stronger.

From the very start of this journal, my plan was to conclude on September 24, the day Carol moved on from this world. I went into this journal open-minded without any preconceived notions, expectations, or anticipated epiphanies. I wanted to keep what I wrote simple and pure to the very *essence* of what I was experiencing. Open to the honesty of the moments I encountered no matter how brutal, embarrassing, or raw and I prayed to be brave enough to share my process, my discoveries, and my vulnerability. I don't know if I would have been capable months ago to even be aware of what I was feeling as I was simply trying to survive the shock of Carol's death and navigate my way through the grief, pain, and sudden new reality.

I believe everyone has their own process for dealing with grief and there is no right or wrong approach. In fact, it's not an approach at all but a debilitating pain and sadness that puts you in a horrible reality you didn't expect ...or want. *Instantly.* This unknown reality you were just dropped into will certainly test you in ways you can't possibly be ready for. Perhaps no human being is ever ready for. Grief forces you to look at the truth of who you are and to discover whether you have the foundation to overcome the overbearing pain and shock that is now your reality. You cannot hide from yourself during this time. For grief, you see, is a painful truth serum. It shows you up close the weakest side of yourself but also brings out the strongest attributes you possess. Attributes you didn't even know you had.

Grief also forces you to be reflective. Remembering the good times you shared is part of the process, but you realize quickly how dangerous it is to linger too long in this reflection because it can trap you and be debilitating. Guilt also introduces itself during this period and reminds you of the times you were insensitive, unappreciative, or simply a jerk. Be careful of this trap as well. Grief is sneaky, it shatters you emotionally and you hold onto the good memories like a drug or life vest. But you can only cling to that life vest for so long.

I believe there are light and dark forces in this world, good and evil that we all encounter in our lives but they truly battle fiercely for your attention during this time. Feeling vulnerable, one can easily fall victim to the many weapons darkness possesses, *despair* being a major one. One realization I had early on came from my three grandchildren, Aiden, Aubrey and Anthony. No matter how much I was in a moment of profound sorrow or despair, the very sight of them, seeing them smile, feeling their embrace, or hearing them call me Pop-Pop, made my heart smile.

We have all heard that life can change in a moment. But when you are dealing with the sudden death of a loved one, everything instantly changes from what you *do* together to what you *did* together. The first question you're confronted with is W*hy did this happen*? Right on the heels of that question is *What could have been done to prevent this*? For me, the question I face today is *What now*? As I've written, it's like being shot in the stomach with a bazooka and looking at the gaping hole in your body, wondering just what the hell happened to you.

When your life partner of thirty-eight years is no longer by your side, the person you loved, who was your confidant, and shared so many life moments, good and bad, how do you continue your own journey without her? You still remain on your own personal journey, but the path has drastically and suddenly been altered. The script you were in has been re-written, and you're *not* the writer. Most of the characters are still in the story, some more than ever, some who disappear. Your character basically remains in tact; however, you are no longer the same person. *How can you be?* There is a new theme, additional sub-plots, and I'm sure some twists and turns still to come as well.

Like a screenwriter with a story to share, I don't know where this story is headed, or where I am headed for that matter. I just have to depend on the truth of myself, the lessons learned from each experience, the love of family and friends, my faith in God, and my willingness to continue exploring the path I am headed toward. I want to be able to write new pages of this new script, hopeful and loving pages filled with exploration and discovery and come out of it somehow a better man. To perhaps even be on a higher path. As of today, although I don't know the ending to this new script, I feel like I am once again able to start writing the story.

I also come away from this year changed mentally, emotionally, psychologically, and spiritually. I should probably add physically as well as I went from weighing 178 pounds to 156 pounds. I didn't want to simply write about my experiences without also sharing what I learned from each encounter, especially to those who are going through the grief of losing a loved one or going through a similar experience. My hope is what I wrote, my challenges, questions, and discoveries, will resonate with them and perhaps, in some small way, offer some peace.

Reading over the journal, I found I used a number of cinematic terms and references to specific scenes, and sometimes felt like I was living those scenes. I guess that is part of my DNA. When you write a screenplay, you start with a central theme and then trust your characters to tell you where to go. In real life, my life, I didn't have a writer putting words in my mouth or a director guiding me on how I am feeling at this moment in this particular scene. I had to trust the same instincts I share with others on a set and apply them to myself, only there were no rehearsals and no one yelling cut when I needed it most.

I also find the similarity between scripts I have written to what I was experiencing during this past year, quite astonishing. I once wrote a screenplay called, *Seasonal Passages* about a man who loses his fiancé in a car accident and how each season reflects his emotional state. My short film *Moments* is the story of a young bride whose husband is killed in war and explores her process toward healing. Were these perhaps premonitions?

I also realized each season brought it's own unique challenges and each reminded me of a personal experience with Carol. In the spring we would always discuss which flowers and plants to buy, the summer was about going out to the house in East Quogue with our family and friends and simple quiet times in the backyard of our new home. Fall would find Carol babysitting Aiden, Aubrey, and Anthony, and hosting many people on Thanksgiving. The Christmas Holidays would always be about Carol making Christmas Eve so special for everyone.

My hope is that anyone reading this journal, not only those who might have lost a loved one and are also grieving, but *anyone* reading this will value their life more and see the people in their lives as absolute *blessings* that should never be taken for granted. Embrace every moment with them, because they can be taken away in an instant. As I mentioned in the journal, I learned that lesson a long time ago from the death of my brother, Frank, but this time was the biggest challenge of my life.

As I was in the early stages of writing the journal, our planet was confronted with a devastating global pandemic, like nothing seen since 1918. It has caused the deaths of hundreds of thousands of people, including my mother, Catherine. Although my life had already been in transition since September 2019, I was once again suddenly confronted with a transitioning world I wasn't ready for. Having to say goodbye to my mother through FaceTime, was another cruel life moment. During the pandemic, I saw an analogy between the planet's transitioning and my own,- two horrible, unexpected, life-altering situations that suddenly drop on you like a building and force you to tap into everything you have learned in your life just to get through another day.

I don't think all the horrible things that have happened in the year 2020 (the notation for perfect vision) are a coincidence. I think the planet is taking a time-out so we can learn a new way to *see* the world and ourselves differently, and to re-evaluate what we *believe* is a priority and what *is* a priority. For me, the pandemic presented an opportunity to, once again, reassess myself and value my life, the people in it, and the people I encounter along the way. To have more empathy that allows me to tap into my humanity and be more appreciative and loving.

I can definitely say that I found a sense of peace and clarity as I wrote the journal. Peace in allowing myself to have an encounter with the sadness and the joyful moments, and a better understanding of my connection to both and what I came away with from each. Often I found these emotions battling for my attention at the same time. Feeling the duality of such strong and opposite emotions simultaneously was startling and confounding, something I didn't realize was possible. This often led to many questions I was confronted with; questions I still have no answers for.

I am grateful for my daughter, Danielle, and my son, Chris, whose love and strength kept me resilient and more grateful than ever to have them in my life. My grand- children Aiden, Aubrey, and Anthony, were light in my darkest moments and made my heart smile no matter how sad I felt. They confirmed that love truly does conquer all. To my daughter-in-law, Melissa, and son-in law, Chris D, for their unconditional love and support. Melissa was also incredibly helpful assisting me manage my Florida properties. I am also blessed to have a wonderful extended family in Larry and Lisa, for always having my back and especially Larry for his financial guidance and to Jeff and Stephanie for letting me know they were only a phone call away and always answered when I called.

I am thankful and grateful for my friends Linda and Kenny and to Stacy and Joanne who shared their own personal journeys of grief losing their husbands and gave me perspective and encouragement to continue writing this journal. I am also grateful to Simonetta, who is always a voice of reason, and my friend Annie who often called and helped fill the empty, lonely hours with conversations, and to my neighbors Ben, Laurie, Gerri and Frank, as well as Gene and Liz, who periodically brought me food, (yes, I became that guy) and invited me to dinners. They all shared a part of their lives and reminded me that fun times with new friends, is still possible.

I am grateful and thankful to my SVA family, Anthony Rhodes for his unwavering loyalty and support, David Rhodes for giving me the time and space I needed to start the healing process, and Gail Anderson and Brian Smith for helping me put together the book cover, and to all my colleagues and friends at the school who took the time to travel and attend the wake and church services for Carol. I was beyond moved. SVA has been a significant part of my life's journey and I am grateful for their loyalty and friendships.

Writing this journal was similar to the scene in the Wizard of Oz: pulling back the curtain and revealing what's *really* hidden behind it, and what's inside of me. Of the many lessons I learned, one of the most important is *You have to be strong in order to be vulnerable.* Strong not only in acknowledging the reality of the sadness you are confronting, but strong in acknowledging the truth of yourself as well. You can't hide from either, you are forced to confront the moment and confront yourself. Once I picked myself up slowly from the ground, I had no choice but to look at the tragic reality in front of me, know it wasn't going away, and see it as the strongest opponent I had ever faced. I had to encounter it with everything I had in order to start the healing process and move forward which also forced me to take a deeper look into myself.

I also discovered that when you suffer the loss of a loved one, if you don't have a strong foundation, you *will* get crushed. There were times when I felt I was holding on by my fingertips and it was only through my faith, my relationship with Christ, my family, and friends (and I needed all of them), that I was able to write and share my thoughts, sadness, and vulnerability.

Throughout the journal, I have written about my relationship with Christ. Writing or speaking about religion, spirituality, or God, often provokes people in both good and bad ways. What I desired to share was not an *ideology* (a word I am not fond of), but simply the truth of my personal experience with God and how I could never have started the road to healing without his presence in my life. I am most human, and most able to see the humanity in people, when I am closest to God.

As my family and close friends know, Carol and I were very different in our personalities and temperament. She was emotional, reactionary, and nervous, yet unconditionally loving, faithful, and nurturing. She was not a *social butterfly* by any means, but to those who were privileged enough to know her, and for those she allowed in, she was the greatest friend. She was a magnificent mother and a devoted and loyal wife. Did we have our differences? The answer would be a resounding yes. Again, anyone who knew us can attest to that. What I always valued was that despite our differences; we had a strong fundamental foundation. We were always free to express ourselves without any fear, personal attack, or lingering bitterness. Writing this journal also showed I loved and valued Carol more than I ever realized.

On our wedding day, as part of the ceremony, we both had to light a candle at the altar. We approached the candle and, together, lit it until the flame glowed brightly. As we turned, the candle inexplicably, died out. The audience reacted and within a few seconds, untouched, the candle re-lights.

I have periodically thought about the meaning of that candle dying out and re-lighting itself over the years. I now believe symbolically this is where I am in this moment of my life, the flame dying out temporarily and magically reigniting itself and shining again.

So here I am, stopped along my journey, no longer sharing this life, this path with my wife Carol, my life mate. I turn around and although she is no longer by my side, I still feel her presence. It's not about moving *on,* but moving *forward.* Although I don't know which path I am heading toward, I feel I am moving in the right direction and can say that now more freely without feeling guilty about it. I just pray that I am strong enough to be heading toward my highest path. I am open to what is ahead and will explore all that is possible. You can't make discoveries without exploring. My desire and curiosity about life and myself, is stronger than ever, as is my passion to continue to evolve and love.

Write what you know, what you have experienced in your life and share it with others. That's what any good film instructor tells their students. Truth really does *resonate,* and moves people in profound ways. Here in this journal, I shared the truth of my experiences during this year of grieving and transition. More than that, I have shared the truth of myself in all its forms. I recognize and embrace more than ever the love that surrounds me and I have accepted and learned the lessons along the way. It is my hope that sharing my personal journey will benefit anyone who has experienced such a loss, or perhaps may feel lost themselves; that would be a good thing.

Though this is the conclusion of the journal, I realize that although my life has certainly changed, it has not ended. It is leading me toward another journey, filled with new experiences, discoveries, and potential. I find myself once again being able to write a new script and open to all its possibilities, or *have I been writing it all along?*

*Thank you, Carol, for your love,*
*and for our life together.*